WILD & WOOLLY WEST

By EARL SCHENCK MIERS

WILD & WOOLLY WEST

Illustrated by Steele Savage

RAND McNALLY & COMPANY
CHICAGO   NEW YORK   SAN FRANCISCO

Copyright © 1964 by Rand McNally & Company
Copyright 1964 Under International Copyright Union by Rand McNally & Company
All rights reserved   Printed in U.S.A.

Library of Congress Catalog Card Number: 64-16834

First printing, 1964
Second printing, 1965
Third printing, 1966

CONTENTS

ILLUSTRATIONS

8

MAPS

1.

LEWIS AND CLARK:
A Race for a Continent

In a sulky mood, President John Adams told the coachman: "Don't spare the horses. Drive hard and drive fast."

Within a few hours Adams would become an ex-President and, in his opinion, by then the country would be well on its way toward going to the devil. Adams was a portly man (foes ridiculed him as "His Rotundity") whose irascible, touchy disposition had so smashed his own party that the Federalists might never again win national office.

How serious this blow could prove to the country was clear to anyone who listened to Adams. Privately he had no great faith in any democracy, and least of all in one that permitted the rabble to send a Thomas Jefferson to the White House. Adams, crouched in the coach with his mouth in a pout, bouncing uncomfortably and staring stoically ahead, had no intention of staying in Washington to see Jefferson's inauguration take place—call it discourtesy, or a snub, or anything you liked.

When, four years before, John Adams had been inaugurated as President, he had worn a sword hung on a sash, a symbol of the pomp that he loved so dearly. The reddish-haired Jefferson, in contrast, affecting garb that identified him with the great mass of people, wore, to his inauguration, clothes so plain that they approached sloppiness. Soon the new President would be shuffling around the Executive Mansion in a pair of old carpet slippers, happily wriggling his toes as he scandalized ambassadors who appeared in fancy uniforms. Perhaps Jefferson's informality was carrying democracy to the point of absurdity—certainly John Adams thought so. Yet even Adams could not deny the strong mind of the man who had followed him into the presidency. A devious, political rascal Jefferson might be, but no one would ever call him stupid.

Of course there were many who went to the other extreme and believed that the Virginian was close to a saint, as political figures were measured. Was he not, after all, the revered author of the Declaration of Independence, who, in the years since, had served his state as Governor, George Washington as Secretary of State, and his country as Vice-President under Adams?

On that March 4, 1801, when Jefferson was inaugurated, he was well aware of the enemies confronting both the country and himself. "Every difference of opinion is not difference of principle," he said, striving to sound a conciliatory note. Meanwhile he had his own notion of what the future must produce.

After two terms of Washington and one of Adams, the United States of America remained painfully young and untested among nations. In the face of erupting regional jealousies and political divisions, just how far the Constitution could be stretched to save the country from itself was an open question. Nor was it any secret in embassies around the world that wise heads were muttering: "With time the United States will fall apart."

Against that happy day, foreign nations already were making certain preparations. Despite the claim of the American navigator Robert Gray, that he had discovered the mouth of the Columbia River in 1792, the British were busily scheming to gobble up all of the Northwest. The Spanish and the Russians had plans for California. And both Spain and France were playing their own little game of cat and mouse in Louisiana to control the mighty old Mississippi, the life line of mid-America.

These were *some* of the problems that bedeviled Jefferson as he rested his carpet slippers on his desk in the White House and reflected on the state of the Union. Somehow all these schemers had to be outwitted. No one knew how vast the wealth of this continent might be, but Jefferson intended to find out. So, even before the prospect of the Louisiana Purchase was a gleam in anybody's eyes, the President called to Washington as his personal secretary, Meriwether Lewis, on detached service with the First Infantry, United States Army.

As an old family friend, educated by the Reverend James Maury, who had been Jefferson's own schoolmaster, Lewis talked the common language of Virginians. Western exploration was fed to them with their mother's milk, more or less, and if expansionism was not part of their political religion, then very little doctrine was.

A month before Jefferson took office, he had offered Lewis a place in his official family—an indication of how carefully he had made his plans. For two years, Lewis familiarized himself with what was on the President's mind before, on January 18, 1803, Jefferson quietly asked Congress for an appropriation of $2,500 "for the purpose of extending the external commerce of the United States." That language, thought Jefferson, should sound harmless to most countries and, to allay the always overactive suspicions of Spain, he proposed to describe the project as a "literary pursuit" intended solely to gather scientific and geographical information.

Congress, in passing the appropriation, knew better: what Jefferson intended was to have an expedition ascend the Missouri River to its source and then go on to the Pacific Ocean. Eyes winked in Washington. Sometimes poker players made the best diplomats.

The most powerful—possibly the most dangerous—international poker player at the time was Napoleon Bonaparte, filled with dreams of a French

empire in the New World. The possession of Santo
Domingo (Haiti) was the key to Napoleon's schemes,
for he saw this island as a center for growing sugar
and other tropical products. To feed his sugar
growers, Napoleon looked toward Louisiana, and the
fact that this territory belonged to Spain hardly
concerned him. Give me Louisiana, Napoleon said
in effect to the king of Spain, and you can have any
principality in Italy you wish.

The deal was made so cosily that Jefferson did not
learn about it until 1802. By then Americans had
become so inflamed over new restrictions on their
trading rights in New Orleans that the President
was forced to send his old friend James Monroe to
France to buy New Orleans, if he could.

But Napoleon was having his troubles in Santo
Domingo—a revolution, an outbreak of yellow fever
—and suddenly went sour on his Caribbean adventure. Moreover, Napoleon at the moment was plot-
ting a war against England, and wars cost money.
So, while Monroe still was at sea, the American en-
voy in France received startling news: the Emperor
was inclined to sell the entire Louisiana territory,
New Orleans included. He offered a bargain, too: for
$15,000,000 Jefferson could acquire over 827,000
square miles along with control of the Mississippi.

For more than one reason the offer was a stun-
ner. No one had ridiculed the Federalists more harsh-
ly than Jefferson for seizing powers not granted by
the Constitution. What authority did the Constitution give *him* to make the purchase Napoleon pro-

posed? The President knew the kind of fuss the New
England Federalists would raise, claiming that in
purchasing territory which doubled the size of the
nation, Jefferson wished only to extend his own ideas
and policies. He knew also that Napoleon could be as
fickle as a schoolgirl and as likely to change his mind.
So Jefferson set aside his principle and accepted
"the noble bargain," and fortunately the Senate sus-
tained the Louisiana Purchase by a vote of 24 to 7.

2.

Now the plan for the expedition under Meriwether Lewis no longer had to be kept secret. In a
long letter of instructions, Jefferson outlined the information he wished concerning the Indian nations
in the unknown West:
"the extent & limits of their possessions;
"their relations with other tribes or nations;
"their language, traditions, monuments;
"their ordinary occupations in agriculture, fish-
ing, hunting, war, arts, & the implements for these;
"their food, clothing, & domestic accomodations;
"the diseases prevalent among them, & the reme-
dies they use;
"moral & physical circumstances which distin-
guish them from the tribes we know;
"peculiarities in their laws, customs & disposi-
tions;
"and articles of commerce they need or furnish, &
to what extent."

The President listed what he believed would be other objects worthy of notice:

"the soil & face of the country, its growth & vegetable productions; especially those not of the U.S.;

"the animals of the country generally, & especially those not known in the U.S.

"the remains and accounts of any which may [be] deemed rare or extinct;

"the mineral productions of every kind; but more particularly metals, limestone, pit coal & saltpetre; salines & mineral waters, noting the temperature of the last, & such circumstances as may indicate their character.

"volcanic appearances.

"climate as characterized by the thermometer, by the proportion of rainy, cloudy & clear days, by lightning, hail, snow, ice, by the access & recess of frost, by the winds prevailing at different seasons, the dates at which particular plants put forth or lose their flowers, or leaf, times of appearance of particular birds, reptiles or insects."

The range of Jefferson's mind—which, as a statesman, philosopher, inventor, and architect would make him so fascinating a man—was never more graphically revealed than in these instructions. He had grown up on a mountaintop, watching the majestic flight of eagles, enraptured by wide vistas, unafraid of the unknown beyond the hazy blue horizon. Now he looked westward across a continent in the same spirit—alert, curious, hopeful, unafraid.

In his old friend Meriwether Lewis the President had been drawn to a man of like intellectual interest, who was a good organizer and administrator, but who possessed a streak of restless, speculative moodiness. Fortunately, as co-leader of the expedition, Jefferson selected William Clark, a younger brother of the George Rogers Clark of Revolutionary War fame. Young Clark always would be remembered by the Indians as "the Red-headed Chief." They grew to love him as a friend and protector with many skills and a sense of humor that was unfailing, who, throughout a long lifetime, was successful and contented in everything he attempted. Two more remarkable men could not have been found. Lewis was twenty-nine years old, Clark thirty-three on that May 14, 1804 when their expedition entered the Missouri River.

They were, indeed, an unusual group. Toussaint Charbonneau, the interpreter, later found an Indian wife and they had a baby. Clark's Negro servant, York, was loved by everybody. So, too, was Lewis's overgrown Newfoundland dog, Scammon. Pierre Cruzatte, blind in one eye and hardly able to see out of the other, proved to be the party's best river boatman and hunter. Soldiers experienced in handling a six-oared pirogue, equipped with supplementary sails, could not have been more valued if their weights had been measured in gold. The wonderful Drewyer (Drouillard) was a Frenchman so gifted as plainsman and riverman, hunter and scout that everything he performed was done superbly. There were also Joseph and Reuben Shields, the

The party started up the Missouri in flatboats—those wonderful craft, piloted by poles and brawn

blacksmiths, and William Bratton, who tinkered with anything until it worked, and brought the expedition through many an emergency. There was some trouble of course—one private sent back for insubordination, another for desertion—but the number of these offenders, really, was small.

3.

The party started up the Missouri in flatboats—those wonderful craft, piloted by poles and brawn, that had opened up the Mississippi and made the Louisiana Purchase essential to national destiny. The journals and letters of Lewis and Clark now were filled with marvelous stories—of the crosscurrents that made the Missouri a treacherous river, of snakes, and ticks, and mosquitoes that could come near maddening a man, of "the great river of the Kansas" whose bottom was choked with willows and cottonwoods, of an Indian powwow at a site that they called Council Bluffs, of poor Charles Floyd who died of a ruptured appendix and was buried beneath "a red ceeder post," of cactus and buffalo herds and prairie dogs living in villages, of tribes known as the Cheyennes, the Arikaras, the Crows, the Minnetarees, of sudden bitter-cold rains and snowstorms that had brought Clark low with an attack of rheumatism.

Faithfully the party carried out Jefferson's "instructions" and the White House became cluttered with the trophies they sent back. In three cases came a burrowing squirrel, a prairie hen, four magpies. A stuffed male and female antelope, with their skele-

Indians of various tribes. From left to right: Mandan, Crow, Cheyenne, Sioux, Minnetaree

tons, was another prize. Now Jefferson could show off to visitors the horns of a mountain ram, or a buffalo robe depicting a battle fought eight years ago by mounted Sioux and Arikaras against the Mandans and Minnetarees. Skins of the red fox, white hare, marten, and yellow bear were other trophies that scouts brought to St. Louis for shipment to the White House. There was also a box of plants, another of insects.

By the time the Lewis and Clark Expedition returned to St. Louis on September 23, 1806, it covered nine thousand miles and became a journey like few in the history of man. Sometimes its story would be one of futility, as when the party set out in quest of the fabled dwarfs of Missouri, with heads eighteen inches high, who were reputed to enjoy killing Indians. Sometimes its story would be one of high adventure, as when the party discovered unsuspected marvels of nature like the source of the Bitterroot River, which, branching off into other streams of breath-taking beauty, led the explorers at last to the great Columbia and on to the Pacific.

Sometimes the story would be one of unselfish heroism as when, approaching the Rocky Mountains, they met Sacagawea, the sister of an influential Indian chief, whose name in English meant "Bird Woman." Born among the Shoshone and Snake Indians in the country later known as Idaho, Sacagawea had been captured by another tribe and sold to Toussaint Charbonneau, the interpreter. She was ill, from giving birth to a son, when Lewis eased her pain with a powdered rattlesnake rattle. The woman's face, alight with gratitude, bespoke the favors she would later bestow upon the party, for her infant son, Pomp, howled lustily, a sound to warm any mother's heart.

Understanding how little any white man knew of the language of the Shoshones, Sacagawea, as a guide and an interpreter, led the Lewis and Clark party across the Rockies to the coast of Oregon. How much of her story is myth, how much history, no one can say, but at the same time no one can deny that she found edible roots whose presence was unsuspected or that she recognized landmarks from her travels and so carried the white explorers over trails they might never have discovered.

All through early November, 1805, the journal that Clark kept was filled with references to fog, to cloudy weather, to rain, but on November 7 came a happy entry: "Great joy in camp we are in *view* of the Ocian, this great Pacific Octean which we have been so long anxious to See." Even though Clark declared that the "roreing or noise made by the waves brakeing on the rocky Shores" could be heard distinctly, his information, like his spelling, was somewhat in error. Clark was camped near Pillar Rock, from where the ocean cannot be seen. But the first glimpse of the Pacific was near—the wonderful achievement of Lewis and Clark, charting a course westward to empire, was almost won.

4.

A pattern had been set. Other explorers under Lieutenant Zebulon M. Pike, striking out from St. Louis, added to America's knowledge of the continent on which it roosted like a mother hen. Pressing up the Mississippi beyond the mouth of the Minnesota River, in 1805 Pike talked with the Indians, established the authority of the United States Government, and selected the site for Fort Snelling (called Fort St. Anthony until 1825). A year later Pike pushed through the Pawnee country and gave his name to Pike's Peak in the Rocky Mountains.

Not more than five years had passed since the day when, in a sulk, John Adams, soon to become the second ex-President of the United States, had

AMERICAN EXPLORATIONS IN THE FAR WEST

Meriwether Lewis and William Clark, 1804–1806

━━━━━━━━━━━ Westward bound

━━▶━▶━━ Homeward bound

Zebulon Pike, 1806

▬ ▬ ▬ ▬ ▬
◀

Louisiana Purchase, 1803

▨▨▨▨▨▨ Indefinite boundary

*The indefinite southwest boundary of the Louisiana Purchase
was changed in 1819 to the definite boundary shown.*

asked the coachman to drive him hastily beyond the limits of Washington City. Now the Louisiana Purchase, bought for about two and a half cents an acre and doubling the size of the Union, was a reality.

But more had happened, for which the nation could thank red-headed Thomas Jefferson: despite the power of Great Britain, Spain, or France, the United States had believed that it must secure its own destiny, and had sent a talented group of men westward for that purpose. On reaching the summit of the peak that bears his name, Zebulon Pike wrote: "Arose hungry, dry, and extremely sore from the inequality of the rocks on which we had lain all night, but were amply compensated for toil by the sublimity of the prospect below." Pike saw an "unbounded prairie" below, "overhung with clouds, which appeared like the ocean in a storm" with "wave piled on wave and foaming, whilst the sky was perfectly clear where we were."

Perhaps the real proof of Thomas Jefferson's genius came, not only in his choice of good soldiers, good scientists, good scholars to find their way to the empire in which he believed, but also in the fact that he selected good poets. Truly, as he informed the minister from Spain before the Louisiana Purchase, our exploration of that region—which today we call affectionately the wild and woolly West—was almost "a literary pursuit."

Yet the fact that the whole picture changed, radically and quickly, may have been due less to Jefferson than to a creature known as *Castor canadensis*.

2.

THE MOUNTAIN MEN:
Trail Blazers of an Empire

Not by any standard could you call the hero of this story a beauty. A good one-third of its body was scaly tail, and some pioneers believed that this rudder-like apparatus gave the Indian the idea for his first canoe paddle. Other features of this fellow, who became one of the most compelling forces in shaping the history of the wild, woolly West, were scarcely more attractive—the furry body, the webbed hind feet, the mustachioed snout, the watery eyes, the protruding front teeth that have been known to gnaw through trees forty-two inches in diameter. Such, in portrait, was the beaver—or *Castor canadensis*—and such was its charm, that grizzled trappers followed its trail west into the Rocky Mountains and on to the Pacific, blazing new paths to empire. (See map, page 22.)

There was nothing that you could tell a mountain man about this rascal. That tail, in addition to serving as a rudder, was also a balancing device when a beaver ran or galloped, a prop for sitting, and a flapper for slapping the water, when a beaver wished to warn other members of the colony of impending danger. On the average, these fellows ran to thirty or forty pounds, although adults often weighed fifty or sixty pounds, and occasionally a trapper stumbled on an old grandfather beaver that had reached one hundred pounds. The flesh, some said, was not half-bad eating, and others swore that it was downright delicious, but then you had to reckon if maybe *they* had been living too long on buffalo meat, which sometimes could be tougher than whalebone.

In their own way, as engineers and prodigious workers, the beavers were nature's masterpiece. They were bark-eaters—these furry busybodies—who stored their winter food underwater in the mud, chewing off the bark and using the stripped logs to strengthen their dams when spring came. The dam, a marvel in its own right, kept the water in the pond at a level where it could not freeze when snows swirled and icy winds blew. Up against the bank was the mud burrow or conical lodge, usually six or seven feet in breadth, where the beaver family lived. Frozen solid in winter, these mud houses were so strong that nothing less than a bear could put its foot through.

Of course, what the mountain man truly admired about the beaver was its fine, shining pelt. Free that pelt from the few long hairs scattered through it, and the remaining fur was close and fine,

As engineers, the beavers were nature's masterpieces

and worth from four to six dollars a pound. "Hairy bank notes," the mountain man called these skins, turning them in for all manner of luxuries, including that rot-gut brand of alcohol with which trappers liked to fire the linings of their bellies and which so emboldened the spirit (or so rumor insisted) that one nip could lead a rabbit to bite a rattlesnake.

What made the trapping business so profitable in the years from 1820 to 1840 was the craze for beaver hats that swept the country and reached to such far-off places as London and Paris. As a result, advertisements, like the one appearing in the *Missouri Republican* for March 20, 1822, were not uncommon:

> TO ENTERPRISING YOUNG MEN. The subscriber wishes to engage one hundred young men to ascend the Missouri River to its source, there to be employed for one, two, or three years. . . .

The "enterprising young men" most certainly did appear, and while few of them ever had much money to show for their years in the mountains, the Old West would never be able to forget, or to thank them from too full a heart, for what they achieved. They were the men who learned where the mountains started and stopped, and how far the deserts stretched, and where rival Indian territories crisscrossed. They were the first to tramp through the Mexican-held lands from Santa Fé to California, and to demonstrate that young George Washington had not been altogether accurate when he had written in his school copybook that "Calofornia" was one of the "Chief Islands" of North America.

To contradict the then prevalent notion that beyond Missouri stretched only a desert waste filled with rattlesnakes and deadlier Redskins, they were the men who stumbled on the almost unbelievable wonders of a vast continent—men like Joseph Reddeford Walker, holding a rifle in one hand and a Bible in the other as, breathlessly he became the first white man to behold the beauty of the valley of the Yosemite; and wrinkled old Jim Bridger, who discovered the Great Salt Lake (map, page 22); and Jim Baker, with his fiery red beard, who outlived six Indian wives and probably crossed as many unknown mountain passes.

Kit Carson was of this breed. At sixteen, sandy-haired, somewhat runty, and plagued with a girlish voice, Kit was toiling as a saddler's apprentice when the lure of the trail led him to run away. As a sign of his contempt for Kit, his employer offered a one-cent award to anyone who would bring him back. For two years, Kit drifted from Santa Fé to Taos (map, page 22)—"Touse," the mountain men called it—doing odd jobs and admitting he "was too small to set a trap." Somehow he must have learned this art for, at nineteen, he connected with an outfit and shot his first Apache—the beginning of the Kit Carson legend that would make his name almost holy among mountain men.

But Kit deserved his reputation. He was the symbol of a fabulous age: he saw the fur hunters come and go; then the missionaries and explorers; then the immigrants, and soldiers, and miners; he saw the prairie schooners raising dust along the Santa Fé Trail, the Oregon Trail, the California Trail (map, page 74); he saw the cowboys driving their longhorns up from Texas, and the sheepherders stringing their wire across the range; he saw so many new states added to the Union that he doubtless lost count; and when the Iron Horse chugged eastward from the Wyoming Rockies, Kit was aboard, to prove that he liked to finish what he started.

2.

All of these events, of course, were part of an undreamed-of future for Kit, riding out of Taos at the age of nineteen, and hoping he could get the better of his girlish voice. No doubt he soon looked like every other mountain man. To catch a glimpse of one of these fellows, jogging along on a shaggy horse, up among the snowy peaks or along the banks of a stream so crystal-clear that it seemed to sparkle with diamonds, was to know him at once by the marks of his trade. There was always a big-bored rifle resting crosswise on his saddle, and a pistol, knife, and toma-hawk squeezed under his belt. His wide felt hat—a godsend when riding the sagebrush plains under a broiling sun—gave emphasis to the long hair that fell around his shoulders. If his leather shirt and pantaloons looked as stiff as boards—well, they were, considering how often they had been smeared with bear grease.

There were also physical characteristics about

this mountain man that were unfailing. His ears never lost a kind of pricked-up alertness, for the sounds of Indians, buffalo herds, and grizzly bears could mean life or death. His eyes came to possess a kind of perpetual, watchful squint, together with a hint of melancholy, for sometimes years passed before he was reunited with his family. In the meanwhile he might take up with some Indian squaw, figuring that this was his business, and when, after fourteen years, Kit drifted back to Missouri, he brought a half-breed son with him.

By then Kit's bones and muscles probably ached all the time, but a mountain man knew this was the price he paid for wading icy streams and climbing rocky trails. He shrugged, mounted his shaggy horse, and pressed on from one beaver colony to the next in quest of those "hairy bank notes." Whether you were Kit Carson or "Old Solitaire" Bill Williams, the devout Joe Walker, or the profane Jim Bridger, the game then was to match wits against the crafty rascals in the pond. In *The History of the American Fur Trade of the Far West,* Hiram Martin Chittenden described every move a Kit or an "Old Solitaire" would make in such moments:

> The universal mode of taking the beaver was with the steel trap, in the use of which long experience had taught the hunters great skill. The trap is a strong one of about five pounds' weight, and was valued in the fur trade period at twelve to sixteen dollars. The chain attached to the trap is about five feet long, with a swivel near the end to keep it from kinking. The trapper, in setting the trap, wades into

the stream, so that his tracks may not be apparent; plants his trap in three or four inches of water a little way from the bank, and fastens the chain to a strong stick, which he drives into the bed of the stream at the full chain length from the trap. Immediately over the trap a little twig is set so that one end shall be about four inches above the surface of the water. On this is put a peculiar bait, supplied by the animal itself, castor, castorum, or musk, the odor of which has a great attraction for the beaver. To reach the bait he raises his mouth toward it and in this act brings his feet directly under it. He thus treads upon the trap, springs it and is caught. In his fright he seeks concealment by his usual method of diving into deep water, but finds himself held by the chain which he cannot gnaw in two, and after an ineffectual struggle, he sinks to the bottom and is drowned. Not infrequently he wrests the chain from the stake, drags the trap to deeper water before he succumbs, or, taking it to the shore, becomes entangled in the undergrowth.

Trapping seasons varied. The spring and fall were the only profitable periods for taking beaver in the northern and central Rockies. A trapper who wanted to work through the winter headed into those parts of the Southwest where there was little ice or snow, and probably ended in Santa Fé, dancing the fandango and gambling away his pelts at monte.

Regardless of the season, one thing was certain —the mountain man always was heading somewhere *else* and discovering rivers that no one suspected existed: the Gila in portions of Arizona, the Colorado with its treacherous currents and awesome canyons, the Humboldt (originally Ogden's River) in

Nevada, the Virgin and the Sevier, the Green and the San Juan in Utah, the Snake and the Bear in Wyoming. Or, like Jedediah S. Smith, a New Yorker transplanted to the mountains, he gritted his teeth and discovered, in 1827, after days of agonizing struggle, the Great Salt Desert. Too soon this legendary scholar of the mountains died, for he had hoped to give the world an atlas of the western country.

3.

If, on entering the Indian country, a Kit Carson or a Jedediah Smith added a deerskin overshirt to cover his body from chin to thigh, he was only exhibiting good sense. Soaked in water and wrung dry, this garment became almost as effective as medieval armor in deflecting arrows.

Every trail posed its own Indian hazards. On that oft-traveled trail from St. Louis to Santa Fé, a trapper crossed the territories of the Osages, the Kiowas, the Pawnees, the Comanches and the Apaches (see map, Chapter 1). If he reached Santa Fé without understanding the Indian's mind, he had only himself to blame. It may be stretching the truth to say that aside from the Flatheads in Montana— who were so unlike other tribes that they even looked upon stealing as shameful—there was hardly any Indian the mountain man trusted, but this does not stretch the truth very far. Scalps were lifted by both white men and red, and the only excuse that can explain the trapper's "ha'r raisin' " was his knowledge that an Indian scalp, when offered to a rival tribe, was an excellent item of barter and, above all else, the mountain man considered himself to be a sharp trader.

There was very little about the Indian that Kit Carson and his breed did not come to know as well (and perhaps better) than the dates of their birth. Wrote one of Kit's contemporaries:

> Every tribe of Indians make their arrows differently. The Snakes put but two feathers on their shafts; the Sioux, when they make their own arrowpoints, or buy them, always prefer long, slim points; the Cheyennes, blunt points, sharp on the edges; the Pawnees, medium points; and the Crows, Blackfeet, Utes, Omahas, Ottoes, and Winnebagoes, long points. The Pawnees wrap their arrowheads with elk sinew, the Crows with deer, and the Santees with sinew taken from the inside of the shoulderblade of a buffalo bull.

A mountain man could also identify an arrow by its feathers. A Cheyenne, for example, could not resist turkey feathers until, learning to disguise the source of an attack, he changed his feathers to make it appear that the arrow he had unleashed had been shot by a Pawnee.

So trickery became part of the Indian character as it appeared to mountain men. They could cite the Apache as an illustration of Indian guile. Now and then an Apache went through an elaborate ceremony —digging a hole in the ground, spitting in it, filling it with earth, dancing around it, sticking an arrow in the mound, piling stones on top and painting himself red—all signs that he had spat out his spite, buried his anger, and would like to be at peace. This ceremony was falsely reassuring to an American unless he remembered that the strength of an Apache's arrow was such that it could go through a man's body when shot from a distance of one hundred yards.

The mountain man was only secure when he could live with realities. "The Utes," said Kit Carson, "are the best shots in the country, whether Indian or white," and Kit, who had handled a rifle since he was a small boy, was forced to admit: "Some of the Utes beat me." In the fur country, mountain men always knew where they stood with the warlike Sioux, Blackfeet, and Arikaras—all were fierce and treacherous by nature. They knew where they stood with the Crows, who talked of friendship while stealing horses; and with the Comanches, the most daring riders on the plains, who offered no truce since, in their pride, they had no intention of ever becoming "slaves of the Europeans"; and with the Snakes and the Mojaves who mixed antelope or deer liver with rattlesnake venom to produce the most poisonous arrowheads in North America.

Yet to think of the mountain man and the Indian as eternal enemies was not altogether true, either. Trappers told a story about Jim Bridger, sometimes called the "Daniel Boone of the Mountains," who was the first explorer of the region that is now Yellowstone National Park. Jim, unable to speak the language of either the Sioux or the Cheyenne, still held both groups spellbound for more than an hour. Said a witness: "The simultaneous exclamations of surprise or interest, and the occasional bursts of hearty laughter, showed that the whole party understood not only the theme, but the minutiae of the pantomime exhibited before them."

Next to Indian treachery the mountain men most feared bears—grizzly, gray, or white—for these shaggy monsters, often weighing well over one thousand pounds, could be as mean-tempered as rogue elephants and a match for even a bull buffalo. "They no sooner see you than they will make at you with open mouth," wrote one trapper. "If you stand still, they will come within two or three yards of you, and stand upon their hind feet, and look you in the face; if you have fortitude enough to face them, they will turn and run off; but if you turn they will most assuredly tear you to pieces." Kit Carson, chased by two grizzlies, admitted that he spent a long time up an aspen tree, and called it the "worst difficult" of all his experiences as a mountain man. Others told of seeing as many as two hundred grizzlies on the plains at one time, a sight guaranteed to curl a trapper's hair.

In addition to "injuns" and "b'ars," mountain men endured a variety of other hardships: hunger, snow blindness, thirst, prairie fires, snowslides, cloudbursts, disease, blood poisoning, and the madness that followed the drinking of too much raw mountain whiskey. Mosquitoes could be an almost constant torment. For virtually all these complaints

the mountain man relied on a standard remedy—
water mixed with buffalo-gall—and you have his
written word for the fact that this mixture was a
wholesome "exhilirating" drink.

4.

Kit's first job with a company out of Taos made
him a "hired" trapper, who was paid an annual
salary to track down pelts for his employer. A
"skin" trapper might like to think of himself as
more independent, but he really was not: the company supplied his traps and he was expected to sell
his benefactor whatever he caught. There were, of
course, "free" trappers, who worked wherever they
pleased and sold their pelts to whomever they liked,
but increasingly, as the years went on, the beaver
trade became a well-organized business. The struggling giants of the industry became the Rocky Mountain Company, the American Fur Company, and the
British-controlled Hudson's Bay Company. It was
no gentle game these rivals were playing in the wilderness. Edwin L. Sabin, an outstanding authority
of the period, wasted no softening adjectives in describing how the Hudson's Bay Company opposed
its American competitors: "When it must outbid, it
outbid; when it must undersell, it undersold; when
it must play alcohol against blanket, it played; and
when it must crush, it crushed."

Yet, despite hardships and the company-insti-
gated fight for fur, the mountain man also had his

fun, especially after 1825 when General William H. Ashley (he was general of the Missouri Militia and later lieutenant-governor of the state) introduced the "rendezvous" among Rocky Mountain trappers. These meetings usually occurred between the middle of June and the middle of September, when the beavers were shedding their furs and their skins were of little value. Whether the trapper headed for Pierre's Hole, the Bear River Valley, the Powder River Valley, or that most favored of all meeting places, the Green River Valley, the rendezvous was his holiday. Washington Irving supplied a picture of a Green River Valley rendezvous in 1832:

> The leaders of the different companies . . . mingled on terms of perfect good-fellowship, interchanging visits and regaling each other in the best style their respective camps afforded. But the rich treat for the worthy captain was to see the "chivalry" of the various encampments engaged in contests of skill at running, jumping, wrestling, shooting with the rifle, and running horses. And then their rough hunters' feasting and carousals. They drank together, they sang, they laughed, they whooped; they tried to outbrag and outlie each other in stories of their adventures and achievements. Here the free trappers were in all their glory; they considered themselves the "cocks of the walk" and always carried the highest crests. Now and then familiarity was pushed too far and would effervesce into a brawl and rough-and-tumble fight; but it all ended in cordial reconciliation and maudlin endearment.

Irving's information came secondhand from the

French-born Captain Benjamin Louis Eulalie de Bonneville, who told tall tales on occasion, but in this instance the captain exhibited becoming restraint. The gambling games—euchre, old sledge, monte—were livelier than Irving suggested (a trapper, losing his last pelt, still could offer his last squaw). Shoshone maidens—many of them good-lookers, too—not infrequently bore the responsibility for what Irving artfully described as "temporary jealousies and feuds." Trappers bid high for red blankets, which seemed to exert a special magic in wooing Shoshone hearts. Traders brought caravans of supplies to the rendezvous, and, wrote Irving:

> . . . Now commenced a scene of eager competition and wild prodigality at the different encampments. Bales were hastily ripped open and their motley contents poured forth. A mania for purchasing spread itself throughout the several bands—munitions for war, for hunting, for gallantry, were seized upon with equal avidity—rifles, hunting knives, traps, scarlet cloth, red blankets, garish beads, and glittering trinkets were bought at any price, and scores run up without any thought of how they were ever to be rubbed off. The free trappers especially were extravagant in their purchases. For a free mountaineer to pause at a paltry consideration of dollars and cents in the attainment of any object that might strike his fancy would stamp him with the mark of the beast in the estimation of his comrades. For a trader to refuse one of these free and flourishing blades a credit, whatever unpaid scores might stare him in the face, would be a flagrant affront, scarcely to be forgiven.

Washington Irving's *The Adventures of Captain Bonneville, U.S.A.* was published in 1837, or two years before German-born Adolph Wislizenus, trapping for the Fur Company of St. Louis, arrived at a rendezvous in the Green River Valley. A different aspect of the encampment fascinated Wislizenus:

The Indians who had come to the meeting were no less interesting than the trappers. There must have been some thousands of them. Their tents are made of buffalo hides, tanned on both sides and sewed together, stretched in cone shape over a dozen poles, that are leaned against each other, their tops crossing. In front and on top this leather can be thrown back, to form door and chimney. . . . I visited many tents, partly out of curiosity, partly to barter for trifles. . . . From some tents comes the sound of music. A virtuoso beats a sort of kettle drum with bells around with all his might, and the chorus accompanies him with strange monotone sounds that showed strong tendency to minor chords. A similar heart-rending song drew me to a troop of squaws that were engrossed in the game of "the hand," so popular with the Indians. Some small object, a bit of wood, for instance, is passed from hand to hand among the players seated in a circle; and it is someone's part to guess in whose hand the object is. . . . It is a game of hazard. In this case, for example, a pile of beads and corals, which lay in the midst of the circle, was the object in question. Men and women are so carried away by the game, that they often spend a whole day and night at it. . . .

A rendezvous usually lasted a week. Then the traders packed up their caravans, the Indians pulled down their lodgepoles, the beaver pelts were baled for shipment to St. Louis, saddles were thrown on the backs of the mules, and there were handshakes and backslaps and throaty cries of "God bless you." The Canadians departed first, filling the valley with their sad boat songs. Leave-takings in Mexican, English, and a dozen Indian languages mixed with the crack of the trader's whip or the soft cluck of tongue with which the mountain man communicated to his shaggy horse. By sundown the Green River Valley was quiet, except for the lonesome howl of a wolf, the muffled roar of a buffalo.

5.

Almost invariably the mountain man said "buff'ler," and hunting the "humped-back cows" was an important part of his year's work. There was mighty little anyone could tell a Kit Carson, a "Captain Billy" Sublette, a "German Frapp" Fraeb, a Joe Meek about the vast herds of bison (American buffalo) that roamed the plains. These herds, led by a patriarchal old bull, could number in the thousands, and that fact resulted, as far as anyone could figure, from an instinct for survival. Aside from man (who came later), the buffalo's natural enemies were pumas, wolves, bears. When an attack came, the buffalo quickly formed in a close group with the cows and the young in the center and the bulls on the outer circle offering the defense. There was a majesty to the swiftness, the deftness with which it all happened.

To the western Indian the buffalo provided both
a way of life and his one real industry. When the
Indian hunted bison he wasted almost nothing of the
kill. The buffalo supplied him with food, fuel, clothing, shelter, tools, glue. The mountain man hunted
far more prodigally—for food, some clothing, and
buffalo-gall to mix with water, the cure-all of his
sundry "complaints." The trapper developed his
own style of buffalo hunting and Rudolph Friedrich
Kurz watched him in action:

> . . . The hunters do not use rifle-patches but
> take along several balls in their mouths; the pro-
> jectile thus moistened sticks to the powder when put
> into the gun. In the first place, on buffalo hunts, they
> do not carry rifles, for the reason that they think the
> care required in loading them takes too much time
> unnecessarily when shooting at close range and, fur-

Hunters approach the buffaloes so closely that they do not aim

thermore, they find rifle balls too small. The hunter
chases buffaloes at full gallop, discharges his gun,
and reloads without slackening speed. To accomplish
this he holds the weapon close within the bend of his
left arm and, taking the powder horn in his right
hand, draws out with his teeth the stopper, which is
fastened to the horn to prevent its being lost, shakes
the requisite amount of powder into his left palm,
and again closes the powder horn. Then he grasps
the gun with his right hand, holding it in a vertical
position, pours the powder down the barrel, and
gives the gun a sidelong thrust with the left hand, in
order to shake the powder well through the priming
hole into the touchpan. . . . Hunters approach the
buffaloes so closely that they do not take aim but,
lifting the gun lightly with both hands, point in the
direction of the animal's heart and fire.

Afterward came the feast. The bones were

but point in the direction of the animal's heart and fire

cracked open to get at the marrow—or "trapper's butter"—which was heated in water almost to the boiling point. The buffalo's blood then was stirred in till the concoction approached "the consistency of rice soup." With the addition of salt and pepper —if you will accept the word of Thomas Jefferson Farnham—the trapper now had "a fine dish," although, as even Mr. Farnham admitted, the fare might prove too rich "for some of my esteemed acquaintances, whose digestive organs partake of the general laziness of their habits."

Opinions differed about buffalo meat. The French trapper Charles Larpenteur quoted fellow mountain men as complaining: "If that's the stuff we've got to live on for eighteen months, God have mercy on us!" Though Larpenteur chewed manfully on buffalo meat, he could not reduce it to a "swallowing condition," and added: "I would seize an opportunity to spit it into my hand, and throw it out unseen behind me." But Farnham would tolerate no derisive talk about buffalo meat, and most of all about stuffed buffalo intestines which, when properly seasoned and roasted (or so Mr. Farnham insisted), found the trapper sitting down to his meal "with as fine an appetite as ever blessed a New-England boy at his grandsire's Thanksgiving Dinner." What such disputes doubtless proved was the fact that, aside from the technique for trapping beavers, mountain men rarely agreed completely over anything, whether the argument involved buffalo meat or Shoshone maidens.

When the ice and snow of a Rocky Mountain winter approached, many could reach another point of agreement: now was the time to tramp over mountain and desert to the gay life in sunny California. Kit Carson, still a greenhorn kid, made his first trip "thataway" in 1829-30.

By now, however, Kit had spent enough time in Santa Fé and Taos to know the sometimes easy-going and always unpredictable habits and customs of the legal inhabitants of Mexican-held territory. All Mexicans looked upon themselves as "whites," which, of course, gave them the privilege of holding the Indians in eternal slavery or peonage. The women stained their faces crimson with the oily juice of the algeria plant—for what reason, Kit never quite fathomed. They all liked to doze, to smoke corn-husk cigarettes, to drink "Taos lightning," to dance the fandango, to go to church (the doors of which were sometimes decorated with Apache scalps as well as the images of saints), and to look upon Americans as rascals who had only one reliable motive: to steal their land and the ugly one-story, mud-brick houses in which they lived.

Striking out for California, Kit learned a great deal—about the proudly independent Navajos, who were properly called the "lords of New Mexico"; and about the Zuñi Indians, who were reputed to be white (and were not); and about the Apaches, in the Arizona of the future, who roamed the Southwest as unknowing as Kit that the land beneath their feet was worth $500,000,000 in gold, silver, and copper. Over mountain and desert, the unfolding landscape was all a miracle to young, wide-eyed Kit. He reached California and its missions with a fluttering heart, like so many other Americans who would come into this romantic region by various routes.

Another, who would make the journey by sea, was Richard Henry Dana, Jr., author of *Two Years Before the Mast,* who visited California in 1836-37. Dana was speaking of old Monterey, the seat of the Mexican government in California, when he referred to the mountain men flocking to "a great place for cockfighting, gambling of all sorts, fandangos, and every kind of knavery." Dana found it a scandal how the trappers and hunters, reaching Monterey with their valuable furs, were "entertained with every sort of amusement and dissipation until they had wasted their time and money" when they started the hard trek back into the mountains, "stripped of everything."

The picture was not precisely fair, for within another ten years the Americans wrested California from the Mexicans.

But that is another story.

3.

LONE STAR AND GRIZZLY BEAR:
The Winning of California

The Monterey that Dana visited in the middle 1830's was as Mexican as the fandango. Four lines of one-story plastered buildings surrounded the open square with its half-dozen ancient cannon. About eighty soldiers, looking ragged and poorly fed, lazily strolled this presidio or fort, that was, in truth, completely unfortified.

Yet the shabbiness of the soldiers somehow blended with the houses, constructed of large clay bricks that had been baked in the sun, and all of which, in Dana's descriptive phrase, possessed a "common dirt-color." Through grated windows without glass, and doors that were seldom shut, the visitor looked in on earthen floors, upon two or three little rooms furnished "with a bed or two, a few chairs and tables, a looking glass, a crucifix of some material or other, and small daubs of paintings . . . representing some miracle or martyrdom."

The warm climate made chimneys or fireplaces unnecessary, and the cooking was done in a small structure separated from the house. A few homes, belonging to the wealthier members of Monterey so-

One-story plastered buildings surrounded the open square with its half-dozen ancient cannon

ciety, had glass windows and red tiles on the roofs.

If drabness set the tone of the town, gaiety marked the style of the people. The women adorned themselves in mantles, gilt necklaces, large earrings, spangled satin shoes, and silk gowns. "They used to spend whole days on board our vessel, examining the fine clothes and ornaments, and frequently made purchases at a rate that would have made a seamstress or waiting maid in Boston open her eyes," Dana wrote.

A drop of Spanish blood was enough to lift an inhabitant above the slave status of the Indian, and Monterey, with its quadroons and octoroons, was acutely class-conscious. Rank could be guessed by complexion, ranging from brunette Castilians to those "growing more and more dark and muddy." Gentlemen who could call themselves *Españolos,* and thus could own property, dressed the part in boots, hat, cloak, spurs, long knife, and a suit of clothes (usually coarse and dirty). Silver and hides were the only forms of money to be found. Clumsy ox carts filled the roads with clouds of dust.

The California that Dana beheld dated its acquaintance with the white man from 1542, when Juan Rodríguez Cabrillo, a Portuguese navigator employed by Spain, sailed into San Diego Bay and explored the coast line and the larger islands in the Santa Barbara group. Cabrillo died before he could report on his discoveries, and romantic tales brought back by his crew, of an island of black women whose arms were covered with gold, did not impress the Spanish authorities.

Then Sir Francis Drake in his *Golden Hind* sailed into San Francisco Bay in 1579, showered gifts of feathers and tobacco on the Indians, and claimed California for England. This challenge was enough to awaken dormant Spanish interest, but when, in 1602, the explorer Sebastián Vizcaíno sent the king an enthusiastic report, urging the immediate colonization of California, it was perhaps consistent with Castilian indolence that more than a century and a half passed before, in 1769, an expedition under Captain Gaspar de Portolá established forts at the sites of San Diego and Monterey.

Over the next half century, some twenty missions were built from San Diego to Sonoma, giving the Indian a choice between the cross or the sword as he was reduced to the subservient role of tending the mission's herd and hoeing its gardens.

When, in 1821, Mexico broke away from Spain, the first measure of self-government reached California under the benign influence of a new kind of colonist, the *ranchero,* who worked hard, laughed heartily, and gave back freedom to the Indians. But even the good heart of the *ranchero* could not soften the suspicions or the arrogance of the typical Mexican government official—jealousy and a quick temper were his stock in trade, bickering his hobby, and slyness as essential to him as his siesta.

Nothing so excited these traits in the Mexican authorities as the sight of *Yanquis* like Dana in their China-bound trading ships, or mountain men like Kit Carson who loped down the mountain sides in search of a little deviltry. No one could ever convince the Mexicans that it was not part of American design to grab all of California the first chance it had, and, if the truth be told, these dark misgivings were not without foundation.

As early as 1835 President Andrew Jackson began sounding out the Mexican government on the cession of San Francisco Bay and succeeded, finally, in stirring up a diplomatic hornet's nest. A visit to San Francisco in the fall of 1841 by an American naval expedition under Lieutenant Charles Wilkes did not comfort Mexican nerves, despite Wilkes's insistence that his only interest was in advancing various branches of science.

A kind of comic exploit occurred the following year when that enterprising American commodore, Thomas ap Catesby Jones, cruising with the Pacific Squadron in Peruvian waters, heard not only that the United States was at war with Mexico but also that Mexico intended to cede California to Great Britain rather than permit it to fall into the hands of the detested *Yanquis.* To say the least, Commodore Jones was a man of action for, without orders, he sailed straight for Monterey.

No port could have looked less warlike. The soldiers were off working in the fields, the fort was falling apart and the guns rusting, the ladies were pinning up their hair with high combs, and the Indians were dozing peacefully in the sun, but Jones stormed ashore, baffled the inhabitants with a firm proclamation, and hoisted the American flag over the presidio. Then Jones learned that there was no war, apologized, hauled down his flag, and established a high mark in diplomatic embarrassment.

But Governor Mitcheltorena was not a hard man. He threw a grand ball for Jones that was "well and brilliantly attended." After all, to err was human.

2.

Even so, 1842 was the year when Mexico had good reason for increasing fretfulness over American intentions toward California, for John Charles Frémont was completing the reconnaissance of trails to the Rocky Mountains that would be the preliminary to his five expeditions across the Great Basin to the Pacific coast. As Frémont stood on the threshold of his enduring fame as the "Pathfinder of the West," it should have surprised no one that beside him stood Kit Carson, that indestructible hero of almost all the epics of the Old West.

The pair met on the boat that was carrying Frémont from St. Louis to the mouth of the Kansas River. Frémont then was twenty-nine, or four years Kit's junior. The explorer was of a dashing French Creole type with flashing blue eyes and waving brown hair, a quick manner and a dominant personality. He made a good impression on everyone. But Kit apparently had matured since his runty youthfulness in Santa Fé. "I was pleased with him and his manner of address at this first meeting," Frémont wrote in his *Memoirs*. "He was a man of medium-height, broad-shouldered and deep-chested, with a clear steady blue eye and frank speech and address; quiet and unassuming.''

Frémont engaged Kit's services for one hundred dollars a month—good wages for that time—but more important was the generosity with which Frémont wrote of Kit, creating in large part the public image on which his fame rests. Of course, as one biographer points out, where could anyone find a more alliterative name than Kit Carson to popularize, unless it was the name of Buffalo Bill?

Frémont's gift with the pen surely was always one of his better virtues. His flowing narrative, his fine descriptions of nature—whether he was speaking of the poppies of early spring or a howling storm in the Sierras—made thousands of stay-at-home Americans fascinated with the country he saw. They followed him almost breathlessly as he went westward by way of the South Platte, Bent's Fort, the South Pass, the Great Salt Lake, and Fort Hall to the Columbia; then southward from The Dalles through the Great Basin (or ''Great Sandy Desert'' as the mountain men called it) across the Cascade Mountains to the Carson River, and so onward across the mountains to California. (See map, page 74.)

Some found Frémont too talkative on the trail, too headstrong, and too hard to get along with. Perhaps he was. They told a story of what happened when Frémont reached the Platte—that river mountain men considered the most magnificent, useless river in America since it was ''a thousand miles long and six inches deep.'' '' He thought he could do anything," they said. "We all told him that he couldn't run the Platte in that rubber boat and when he upset we were tickled."

Doubtless they were, but Americans at home, thrilling to Frémont's narrative of how "without a saddle, and scouting bareheaded over the prairies, Kit was one of the finest pictures of a horseman I have ever seen," were drawn to Frémont, the Far West, and, in time, to California. Congress was never slow in voting the funds for another Frémont expedition. He had become permanently woven into the fabric of the American imagination.

Frémont's first visit to California came in the winter of 1843-44. Traveling trails, Frémont said, that could be described only as "rock upon rock— rock upon rock—snow upon snow—snow upon snow," he came at last to the beautiful Sacramento Valley and Sutter's Fort.

The romantic John Augustus Sutter should have entranced Frémont. This Swiss–German emigrant, reaching New York, in the summer of 1834, without a penny, had struck off for the mountains of New Mexico and Colorado, journeyed to Oregon, Hawaii, Alaska, and so, by his own impractical route, had come in time to San Francisco. Then, hopeless dreamer or super-salesman as you like, he had persuaded the Mexican governor to give him five thousand acres in the Sacramento Valley to found a principality that he intended to call New Helvetia. With an odd crew of "sailors, Kanakas, Mexican cowboys and friendly Indians," Sutter proceeded to make his dream come true. He was a dynamo of human energy, whether digging wells, running pipes from the river, laying out fields, throwing bridges across streams, or building the fort that bore his name. Ultimately his fame would rest on a piece of luck that he never anticipated.

During Frémont's two-week stay at Sutter's Fort, his ears perked up at rumors of a rising spirit toward independence, as increasing numbers of Americans emigrated into California. The country was without proper military defense, he learned, and there was persistent talk of British schemes to annex the territory. All these rumors Frémont carried back to Washington, and each, almost certainly, became a sizable flea to lodge in the ear of influential Senator Benton, who was Frémont's father-in-law.

Soon the Pathfinder was heading westward on his second scientific expedition and discovering on his next visit to Sutter's Fort that his relations with José Castro, the commanding general, were somewhat strained. Frémont received permission to winter in California as long as he kept away from the coastal settlements, a clear indication of whither Castro's suspicions were directed, and so it should have come as no great surprise that Castro's anger flared when he found Frémont's party marching through the Salinas Valley.

Castro ordered the Pathfinder to get out or suffer the consequences, and Frémont, in a huff, moved to Hawk's Peak, which commanded the surrounding plain, and defied Castro to throw him out. For three days the affair amounted to a glaring contest without bloodshed; then Frémont, his face saved, started up the Sacramento Valley toward Oregon. The Hawk's Peak incident had its significant undertones, strengthening the belief that, if revolution came, Frémont could be counted upon to forget science for the sake of an appropriate uprising.

A surprise attack of Kalmath Indians upon Frémont's camp added to the ugly stories that the Castro forces were encouraging Indians to massacre Americans as part of a well-calculated plan to drive all foreigners out of the province. Frémont came back to the Sacramento Valley with his hackles rising. Old John Sutter wished the Pathfinder would go away, for Sutter preferred to live and let live.

Such, however, was not the course of history in that June of 1846. Ezekiel Merritt, gaunt, illiterate and picturesquely described as a "tobacco eater," seized a band of horses being gathered for Castro's use. That was the start of the trail of revolution that ran like wildfire up the Sacramento Valley and burst forth four days later in rebellion at the village of Sonoma. Here a band of settlers, led, among others, by William Brown Ide, who had tried carpentry in New England, school teaching in Ohio and Illinois, and farming in California, seized the village from the Mexicans.

Ide and his followers may have been amateur revolutionists, but they did their work with a becoming flourish, running up an unbleached cotton flag "sufficiently significant of their intentions—a white field, red border, with a grizzly bear eyeing a single star, which threw its light on the motto, 'The Republic of California.' ' "

In addition, on June 15, 1846, Ide issued a proclamation inviting all peaceable and good Californians to assist in establishing "a Republican government which shall secure to us all Civil & religious liberty, which shall encourage virtue and literature, which shall leave unshackled by fetters Agriculture, Commerce & Mechanism." Even in the heat of "battle," Ide could not forget that he had been a school teacher!

3.

Today the Bear Flag, waving over all state buildings as California's official emblem, tends to over-emphasize the importance of the Bear Flag Revolt. Old Sutter looked upon the entire enterprise as work inspired by a "band of thieves," but Frémont seemed exalted. The California Battalion that he led to aid the "Bear Flaggers" was a ragtag

Today the Bear Flag is California's official emblem

group of trappers, scouts, former sailors, frontier farmers, and ranchmen who managed a single skirmish near San Rafael before more pertinent news reached them: the United States was at war with Mexico, a strong American naval force under Commodore John D. Sloat already occupied Monterey, and California was now considered an independent possession of the Washington government.

Of course California's liberation did not work out quite that easily, even though the more aggressive Robert F. Stockton soon replaced Sloat in command of the American naval forces. José Castro recovered his wits, aided unconsciously by the American commander at Los Angeles, Captain Archibald Gillespie, whose arrogant behavior so infuriated the native Californians that they rose in open revolt against the Americans.

So just after Stockton sent Kit Carson across the continent to inform Washington that everything was sweetness and light in California, both Stockton and Frémont were wallowing in disaster. They would have been in even deeper trouble if the remarkable "Lean John" Brown, an old fur trapper destined to become California's Paul Revere, had not ridden almost five hundred miles in five days to rally recruits. Even against these reinforcements, the Californians fought on effectively, aided in no small measure by a cannon called the "Old Woman's Gun" which they fired by applying a lighted cigarette to the touchhole.

Ultimately an exhausted force under Colonel

Stephen W. Kearny, led by Kit Carson from Santa Fé, staggered over the mountains and were saved from extinction in their first battle by the Californians' habit of hit-and-run fighting. Slowly, Stockton, Frémont, and Kearny welded their ragtags together, with assistance from some painted Delawares, into an effective fighting organization, and the end came with the signing of the Cahuenga Capitulations, on January 13, 1847. Californians were simply required to surrender their public arms, pledge to obey the laws of the United States, and refrain from joining the war again on the side of Mexico—a more conciliatory document could not be imagined.

4.

In the annals of the wild and woolly West, the winning of California was truly a climactic chapter, but this was now a story moving in so many directions that it resembled a desert night with the sky full of shooting stars. On that June 15, 1846 when Ide was running up a homemade Bear Flag at Sonoma, the British Minister and our Secretary of State were signing in Washington the Oregon treaty that recognized the forty-ninth parallel as the international boundary from the Rockies to the Pacific. The strokes of their pens thus decided the future of three states: Washington, Oregon, Idaho. On this day 16,000 stubborn Mormons made their first entrance into Council Bluffs, Iowa, on a historic trek that would decide the future of Utah and Nevada. (See map, page 74.)

4.

TRAILS TO THE SUNSET:
Missionaries, Homesteaders, Mormons

After the middle 1830's, the missionary became a familiar figure at a rendezvous of mountain men. Kit Carson's favorite was Father Pierre Jean De-Smet, a Jesuit. "I admire and venerate that good man," Kit said. "He is the only missionary I ever saw who had the slightest effect upon the trappers. All the Indians, even those who have never seen him, venerate 'the long black robe.' I remember he came once among the hunters and trappers up in the mountains, and baptized forty-odd children."

Jim Bridger's favorite was the amiable Dr. Marcus Whitman, who was both surgeon and missionary and who removed from Jim's shoulder an iron arrow left there by a Blackfoot three years earlier. The operation was one requiring great skill, but while Jim gritted his teeth the doctor performed his surgery with superb self-possession, and the Indians looked on with open-mouthed astonishment.

The Reverend Samuel Parker was another popular figure among the mountain men, though he privately lamented the influence of the trappers on the Indians: "It is said that they have sold them packs of cards at high prices, calling them Bibles; and have told them, if they should refuse to give white men wives, that God would be angry with them and punish them eternally; and on almost any occasion when their wishes have been resisted, they have threatened them with the wrath of God."

Despite the domineering manner with which the Hudson's Bay Company conducted its fur business in the Oregon country, the introduction of the "new religion" among the Indians, encouraging the subsequent migrations of the missionaries, was largely its achievement. Every Sabbath the company raised its flag so that the day came to have special meaning among the Indians as "flag day." The company's trappers read the Bible to the Indians and awakened such interest in the Scriptures that when the promise of Bibles for their use was not filled, a spokesman traveled far to lodge vigorous complaint:

I came to you over a trail of many moons from the setting sun. You were the friend of my fathers who have all gone the long way. I came with one eye partly opened, for more light for my people who sit in darkness. I go back with both eyes closed. . . . My people sent me to get the white man's book of Heaven. You took me where you allow your women to dance, as we do not ours, and the book was not there; you showed me the images of good spirits and pictures of the good land beyond, but the book was not among them to tell us the way. . . . When I tell my poor blind people, after one more snow, in the big council, that I did not bring the Book, no word will be spoken by our old men or by our young braves. One by one they will rise up and go out in silence. My people will die in darkness, and they will go on the long path to the other hunting grounds.

Neither the officials of the Hudson's Bay Company nor churchmen in the East who read such appeals could resist this call to religious duty. The missionaries started westward. A Methodist clergyman, Jason Lee, and his nephew, Daniel, were the first to reach the Northwest and, by 1835, had established a mission and school in the Willamette Valley. Dr. Marcus Whitman and Henry Spaulding, with their wives (the first women to cross the continent) arrived the following year.

For all that Henry Spaulding counseled his sponsors back East, "Never send another woman over those mountains, if you have any regard for human life," Narcissa Whitman appeared to take the hard journey in exuberant spirit. Her letters home were filled with the wonder of her trek. Buffalo meat delighted her. She was, she boasted, "a very good housekeeper on the prairie," setting a neat meal on the ground by using an Indian rubber cloth for a cover, tin dishes, iron spoons and forks, and basins for teacups.

"Do not think I regret coming," she wrote. "No, far from it; I would not go back for a world." The Indians, the mountain men fascinated her. She did not deny the hardships, the tedium of one day that was like a dozen others on the trail, but "blessings gather thick around us." Exultantly she arrived in Vancouver, "the New York of the Pacific," happy in her new life. The trials of the trail would never stop women like Narcissa Whitman from following husband and family across a wilderness!

Cheerfully the missionaries adapted to the crude life of the Oregon country, hewing their cabins and barns, their schools and churches from the forest. Newly tilled ground, the surrounding wilderness supplied their food. The climate proved mild, requiring little outlay for stabling or winter foraging of their animals, and that was important in a region where wheat and pelts provided the principal mediums of exchange.

The missionaries set up the first printing press in the Northwest—a gift from fellow missionaries in the Sandwich Islands—and organized the first rudimentary courts and local government. Their letters home attracted others to the Oregon country and the white population swelled when the "Peoria Party" arrived in 1839, a few more settlers the next year, and about forty adults and children in 1841.

2.

Two years later came "The Great Emigration." This was the year when Frémont first reached California. There seemed to be something in the air, calling Americans westward. For those who traveled the Oregon Trail, the jumping-off point was the Platte in Nebraska. To the crack of whip, the rumble of wagons, the braying of cattle, a great column of settlers, numbering over a thousand, moved on. Ten miles a day was a wonderful pace rambling up the North Platte into Wyoming. Summer heat often shriveled the rims of the wagon wheels, the alkali dust kicked up by the six-oxen teams choked those riding behind, but on the pioneers pressed—along the Sweetwater in Wyoming, then across snow-capped mountains through South Pass, and finally down the

On the pioneers pressed—across snow-capped mountains

western slope of the continent to Fort Bridger.

The days were long. At four o'clock in the morning the sentinels fired their rifles, the signal for getting up. Wagons and tents were soon emptied and the air filled with smoke from slowly kindling fires. The herders rounded up the cattle. Peter H. Burnett, who followed the "Great Emigration" to Oregon that year, pictured the bustle:

> From six to seven o'clock is a busy time; breakfast is to be eaten, the tents struck, the wagons loaded, and the teams yoked and brought in readiness to be attached to their respective wagons. All know that when, at seven o'clock, the signal to march sounds, those not ready to take their proper places must fall into the dusty rear for the day.

The wagons moved off in platoons of four, each entitled to lead in its turn. The women and children piled aboard. The pilot was a seasoned mountain man, alert to every sign of Indian deviltry, every sign of wilderness storm. Ten or fifteen men rode ahead, searching for buffalo or the tracks of hostile Sioux. The cattlemen, the horsemen attended their herds, knowing their jobs. As the long day wore on, Peter Burnett was captured by the drama he witnessed:

> The picture, in its grandeur, its wonderful mingling of colors and distinctness of detail, is forgotten in contemplation of the singular people who give it life and animation. No other race of men with means at their command would undertake so great a journey—none save those could successfully perform it with no previous preparation, relying only on the fertility of their invention to devise the means to

overcome each danger and difficulty as it arose. They
have undertaken to perform, with slow-moving oxen,
a journey of two thousand miles. The way lies over
trackless wastes, wide and deep rivers, rugged and
lofty mountains, and is beset with hostile savages.
Yet, whether it were a deep river with no tree upon its
bank, a rugged defile where even a loose horse could
not pass, a hill too steep for him to climb, or a threatened attack of an enemy, they are always found
ready and equal to the occasion, and always con-
querors. May we not call them men of destiny? They
are people changed in no essential particulars from
their ancestors, who have followed closely on the
footsteps of the receding savage from the Atlantic
seaboard to the valley of the Mississippi.

At noon the column rested, the oxen were un-
yoked, the wagons drawn up four abreast. Friends
visited. Sometimes at noon the leaders of the group
met to consider a question in dispute. Such meetings
were called "a council," which Burnett described as
"a high court in the most exalted sense," for its
decisions were final.

Whether or not the council met, the bugle
sounded and at one o'clock the columns moved westward. There was drowsiness now—men slumbered,
awoke with a start, smiled apologetically. Illnesses
were treated at this time, encouragement given concerning the hazards ahead, but meanwhile the wagons rolled on until the sun began to sink and supper
time approached. Then the wagons drew into a circle, fires of buffalo chips were lighted, laughter and
talk filled the air. What followed delighted Peter
Burnett:

The wagons drew into a circle, fires of buffalo chips were lighted, laughter and talk filled the air

It is now eight o'clock when the first watch is to
be set; the evening meal is just over, and the corral
now free from the intrusion of the cattle or horses,
groups of children are scattered over it. The larger
are taking a game of romps; the wee toddling things
are being taught that great achievement that distin-
guishes man from the lower animals. Before a tent
near the river a violin makes lively music, and some
youths and maidens have improvised a dance upon
the green; in another quarter a flute gives its mel-
low and melancholy notes to the still air, which as
they float away over the quiet river seem a lament
for the past rather than hope for the future. It has
been a prosperous day; more than twenty miles have
been accomplished of the great journey. The encampment is a good one. . . .

So drew the day toward its close. The pilot, tired,
sat apart, puffing on his pipe. The members of the
watch went off to their posts; the older men, who had
been meeting in council, broke off and went to bed.
Young men kissed their girls, hating to see the day
end. By ten o'clock everyone was asleep, and the
guards, making their rounds, murmured: "All's
well." Year after year, to the crack of whips and
the rumble of iron-rimmed wheels, the cry of "On
to Oregon" rang out until, by 1846, there were six
thousand Americans in the territory and only one
thousand British.

3.

Not all parties could tell a happy story. George
Donner was sixty-two years of age when, in the
spring of 1846, he sold his prosperous 240-acre farm

in Springfield, Illinois and with his brother Jacob, his little wife, Tamsen, and a group of neighbors struck out for California. The Donner party totaled eighty-seven when, in Utah, they decided to try the newly discovered short cut south of Great Salt Lake. The guide who was supposed to lead the party was never seen, but still the pioneers were determined to find a route over the Wasatch range.

In the succeeding days the men heaved their shoulders against huge boulders, rolling them out of the way. They sweated and swore as their shovels attempted to dig wagonways along treacherous hillsides. Axes slashed at tangled willows. In twenty-one days the party had crept forward only thirty-six miles, and another six days were consumed struggling across the desert.

Each day brought another reason for dark scowls and bitter words: the oxen stampeded; horses and mules were stolen by the Indians; one man was killed in a quarrel; another murdered. Two Indian guides, sent from Sutter's Fort with food (only seven muleloads, a pitifully small supply considering the lateness of the season for crossing the Sierras) warned stoically: "Push on over the mountain. It means death if more snow comes."

At Truckee Lake, in the Sierras, early snows trapped the wanderers. For eight days the white flakes fell almost without interruption and the nights turned bitter cold.

By late November a member of the party, Patrick Breen, wrote in his diary that it was "snowing fast" and added: "No living thing without wings can get about."

The awful truth no longer could be denied: the Donner party was marooned for the winter, without bread or salt and with very little lean beef, most of its cattle and horses lost in the snow, and with knocked-together double cabins or lean-tos as their only shelter against the cruel weather. By early December Peter Breen's diary became crowded with grim entries: "Took in Spitzer yesterday, so weak that he cannot rise without help; caused by starvation . . . Baylis Williams died the night before last . . . Sad news: Jacob Donner, Samuel Shoemaker, Rinehart, and Smith are dead; the rest of them in a low situation . . . extremely difficult to find wood. . . ."

Trapped with the Donner party was Virginia Reed, whose girlhood mind became filled with stark memories:

> The misery endured during those four months at Donner [Truckee] Lake in our little dark cabins under the snow would fill pages and make the coldest heart ache. Christmas was near, but to the starving its memory gave no comfort. It came and passed without observance, but my mother had determined weeks before that her children should have a treat on this one day. She had laid away a few dried apples, some beans, a bit of tripe, and a small piece of bacon. When this hoarded store was brought out, the delight of the little ones knew no bounds. The cooking was watched carefully, and when we sat down to our Christmas dinner, Mother said, "Children eat slowly, for this one day you can have all

you wish.'' So bitter was the misery relieved by that one bright day that I have never since sat down to a Christmas dinner without my thoughts going back to Donner Lake.

The storms would often last ten days at a time, and we would have to cut chips from the logs inside which formed our cabins in order to start a fire. We could scarcely walk, and the men had hardly strength to procure wood. . . . Poor little children were crying with hunger, and mothers were crying because they had so little to give their children. . . .

Patrick Breen's diary bore out Virginia's recollections: ''They have nothing but hides to live on . . . Landrum crazy last night . . . food growing scarce; don't have enough fire to cook our hides. . . .''

Mrs. Reed was not going to watch her children starve—she would cross the mountains herself and bring them bread. Stout-hearted Milt Elliott, in snowshoes, made the tracks for Mrs. Reed, Virginia, and a friend named Eliza to follow. Eliza did not last through the first day and turned back to the cabin with a woeful moan. As Milt, Virginia, and her mother pressed on, they were really crawling rather than walking. Mountains and snow—mountains and snow—that was all they could see.

At night the trees creaked mournfully in the wind, and wolves howled. One morning Virginia awakened in a deep well of snow melted by the camp-fires during the night, and only Milt's steadying voice as, step by step, he dug a path to the surface, saved her life. Virginia sank down in tears, her foot frozen.

Wearily Mrs. Reed admitted defeat. "There is nothing to do but go back," she said.

It was well they did, for heavy snows soon swirled through the Sierras. Virginia lived gloomily through still more days, cooped up in the cabin, watching her mother boiling hides into a kind of soup and thinking, "It looks like a pot of glue!" By mid-February, brave Milt Elliott died in the Murphy's cabin and soon Patrick Breen was writing the grimmest note in his diary: "Mrs. Murphy said here yesterday that she would commence on Milton and eat him. I do not think she has done so yet; it is distressing."

Minds wandered until it was difficult to remember anything clearly. Almost forgotten by now was the relief party—ten men and five women under Charles Stanton—that had struck out for California after Baylis Williams became the first to perish from starvation. "The forlorn hope," Virginia had muttered, watching them start off on their homemade snowshoes. For a month, Stanton's followers struggled on. Eight men died in the snow, but the others, ghostlike and tottering, reached California and poured out their tale of horror in the Sierras.

All that night settlers stayed up killing cattle, drying beef, making flour. A relief party of seven under Captain Reasen P. Tucker left next day, and on the evening of February 19, 1847 found the starving remnant of the Donner party.

Joy welled up in every heart. Saved at last, Mrs. Reed and Virginia dug up the body of Milt Elliott, which they had hidden in the snow, and gave him a proper burial. Poor Milt, they thought, as they prayed sadly—he was only one of many friends who were gone, for of the eighty-seven that left Utah with the Donners, only forty-eight finally reached California.

4.

Hard on the heels of the Donner party came the Mormons, although their story really began in upper New York State where Joseph Smith grew to manhood.

In an age when religious revivals were sweeping this region, causing many converts to "bark like dogs," to exhaust themselves in outbursts of "hopping," and sometimes to fall into cataleptic trances, Joseph Smith believed that the Holy Father and Son appeared to tell him that all churches were wrong. Many times thereafter, Joseph Smith claimed, he was visited by an angel of the Lord who promised that his name would be known "for good and evil among all nations," and who revealed the existence of golden plates or tablets that he was to translate.

These golden plates, Smith said, were delivered to him in 1827 and, for the next two years, "by the gift and power of God," he translated the story and prophecies of ancient Americans of Israelite origin who presumably had lived in the Western Hemisphere from about 600 B.C. to 420 A.D. Smith's work, the *Book of Mormon,* upon which the religion of the Latter Day Saints was based, declared: "We believe

Oregon and California Trails (———) and Santa Fé Trail (----)
discussed in Chapter 2; Frémont's route (xxxx) discussed in

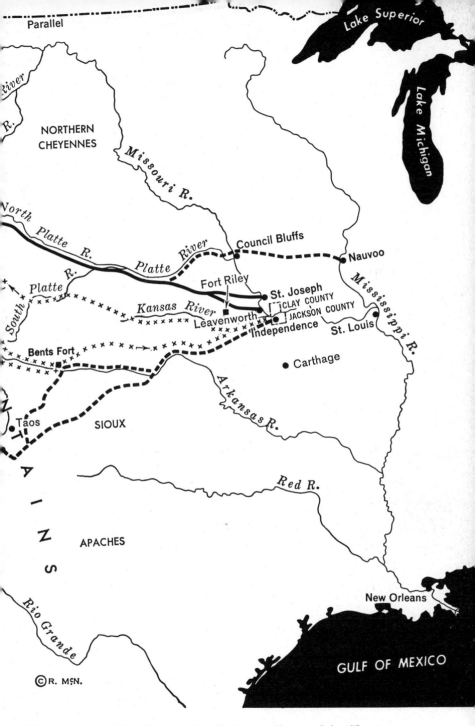

Parallel

Lake Superior

Lake Michigan

NORTHERN CHEYENNES

Missouri R.

North Platte R.

Platte River

Council Bluffs

Nauvoo

South Platte R.

Fort Riley

St. Joseph

CLAY COUNTY

JACKSON COUNTY

Kansas River

Leavenworth

Independence

St. Louis

Mississippi R.

Bents Fort

Carthage

Taos

SIOUX

Arkansas R.

Red R.

APACHES

Rio Grande

New Orleans

©R. McN.

GULF OF MEXICO

Chapter 3; and the Mormon Trail (- - - -) discussed in Chapter
4. Also cities, rivers, etc. discussed in Chapters 2, 3, and 4.

in the literal gathering of Israel and in the restoration of the Ten Tribes; that Zion will be built upon this [the North American] continent; that Christ will reign personally upon the earth; and, that the earth will be renewed and receive its paradisical glory."

Persecuted for their beliefs, Prophet Joseph Smith and his followers moved westward in search of the promised land. In 1831 they settled in Kirtland, Ohio, where the church grew rapidly in membership. The first temple began to rise. But Joseph Smith, visiting Jackson County, Missouri, now decided that Missouri was Zion and, once more, many of the faithful moved westward.

Hard-headed individualists who had no patience with Smith's prophecies—and, moreover, hard-core sympathizers with slavery, which the Mormons opposed—Missourians turned belligerently on the newcomers, driving them from Jackson County into Clay County. But a worse disaster was in store. A sermon by a Mormon leader warning all Missourians "to come on us no more forever" except "at the expense of their lives" found hot-headed Missourians willing to run that risk. A mob fell on the Mormons at Hauns Mill and massacred eighteen. Many leaders, including Joseph Smith, were thrown into jail, providing an opportunity for a brilliant new leader named Brigham Young to come to the fore.

Escaping from prison, Smith rejoined his people and led them into friendlier Illinois country. The little town of Commerce he renamed Nauvoo, "the

Beautiful,'' and within five years made it the largest town in Illinois. Among the forward-looking actions of Joseph Smith was the chartering of the University of the City of Nauvoo, probably the first municipal university in the United States.

But Smith had his weaknesses. He became deeply entangled in political disputes and, in 1844, he set himself up as a presidential candidate. Enemies— some political, some of different religious faiths— began circulating scandalous stories about the debauchery and plural marriages that were taking place in Nauvoo. Local farmers heard that the town was a hang-out for bands of horse thieves. In 1844, the year of Smith's greatest political ambition, the *Nauvoo Expositor* bitterly attacked the management and morality of the Mormons.

Such libelous charges were more than the Prophet could endure. His City Council smashed the press. Protest swept like an angry wave over the surrounding countryside. Smith and his brother Hyrum were jailed in nearby Carthage, where an aroused mob stormed the prison and killed both.

Again the Mormons turned westward, this time under the leadership of Brigham Young, who "spoke with the voice of Joseph." In the winter of 1846 the Mormons reached the west bank of the Missouri and quartered near the site of present-day Omaha. Young, who had read Frémont's exciting reports of the Great Salt Lake Valley, began talking of the "vision" that led him irresistibly toward that region.

Reaching this promised land on July 21, 1847,

The ferry at Council Bluffs, where Brigham Young and his followers crossed the Missouri on their way westward

the Saints fell to work with the dedicated energy that one day would give Utah the nickname of "the Beehive State." The waters of City Creek were turned out of its bed to soften the ground for plowing. Land, water, timber were declared the common property of the community, to be used for the benefit of all. By the end of August the Mormons had broken, watered, planted, and sowed "upwards of 100 acres" with various kinds of seed, had stockaded nearly ten acres, and had constructed a line of log cabins. Truly, the Saints believed in "faith through works."

The following year, however, that faith was sorely tested when a frost in June, withering the young corn, beans, and wheat was followed by crickets "by the thousands of tons." Then, like a miracle, flocks of gulls appeared, devouring the crickets. By mid-July the new wheat was through the ground and a Saint wrote exultantly in his journal: "God has sent us here, and here we are going to stay."

Doubtless "the miracle of the gulls" played a significant role in the settlement of Utah, but more so did the dynamic leadership of Brigham Young. A French visitor to America, Jules Rémay, described the great Mormon at work:

> . . . We found him in his official cabinet, dictating instructions to his secretaries, and at the same time preparing a quid of Virginia tobacco. He occupied an armchair, in which he rather squatted than sat. On his head he wore a broad-brimmed, fawn-colored felt hat. His coat, of greenish cloth, was of the

cut which was called formerly *à la Française,* but of inordinate amplitude. His stockings, visible below his trousers, were clean and white, and his linen tolerably fair. He continued dictating for half an hour, without appearing to take the least notice of our presence. Then, as soon as he had finished, he exchanged a few words with an Indian who had kissed his hand when he entered. Mr. Haws [the interpreter] now presented us to His Excellency. Brigham Young shook hands with us, then retired into an adjourning apartment, from which he returned in about two minutes with a plug of tobacco which he gave to the Indian. He then asked us to take a seat and sat down himself without taking off his hat. . . . He did not appear to pay attention to us and did not condescend to favor us with a word. We learned afterward that we were looked upon as persons of bad character, sent by the Gentiles [a term applied to all non-believers] to assassinate the leader of the Mormons. . . .

The year of Rémay's visit was 1855 and Brigham Young was now fifty-four years of age. Already he had waged his bitter struggle to have "Deseret"— the Indian name for Utah—admitted to the Union. Congress granted territorial status to Utah in 1850, rejecting Young's suggested name, which set up an image in official minds of a "dirty, insect-infested, grasshopper-eating tribe of Indians," but the troubles of the Mormons were by no means ended.

Young's belief that he derived his authority directly from God did not make him the easiest person with whom to deal. Moreover the knowledge that the Mormons practiced polygamy or plural marriages—

that is, that a man could have more than one wife—
chilled the blood of other Americans who believed a
family should consist of one father, one mother, and
their children. Not until 1896, six years after the
Mormon Church outlawed plural marriages, would
Utah be admitted to the Union as our forty-fifth
state. Meanwhile Nevada gained admission in 1864,
Oregon in 1859, Washington in 1889, Idaho in 1890.

5.

So did the empire that the mountain men charted
grow—in California under Carson, Frémont, Stockton; in Oregon, Washington, and Idaho under the
missionaries and settlers who braved the perils of the
trail into the sunset; in Utah, and later Nevada,
under the faithful Mormons who followed the Saints
to Kirtland, to Missouri, to Nauvoo, to the valley of
the Great Salt Lake.

No less certainly was the empire of the mountain
men being molded in the old Southwest. Farms might
lead settlers to Oregon, but the hope of quick profits
drew traders to Santa Fé. Out of St. Louis, a hundred wagons, with merchandise valued at $200,000 (a
tremendous sum for that time), would start their
trek southward. Every type of costume, from the suit
of the city merchant to the buckskins of the back-
woodsmen, could be found in such processions.

"Catch up! Catch up!" ran the cry in the morning
when the trading caravan started. Josiah Gregg, who
traveled with one of the caravans, remembered:

The uproarious bustle which follows—the hallooing of those in pursuit of animals—the exclamations which the unruly brutes call forth from their wrathful drivers; together with the clatter of bells—the rattle of yokes and harness—the jingle of chains —all conspire to produce a clamorous confusion which would be altogether incomprehensible without the assistance of the eyes; while those alone would hardly suffice to unravel the labyrinthian maneuvers and hurly-burly of this precipitate breaking up. . . .

Josiah Gregg, bound for Santa Fé, sounded like the Donner party bound for California, or the Mormons, under Brigham Young, bound for the valley of the Great Salt Lake, when he wrote: "Then the 'Heps' of drivers—the cracking of whips—the trampling of feet—the occasional creak of wheels—the rumbling of wagons—form a new scene of exquisite confusion, which I shall not attempt further to describe."

The scene that Josiah Gregg beheld was no longer "new," and it would become older still when, in 1849, gold was discovered in California.

5.

THE FORTY-NINERS:
And Those Who Came Later

Everything began to happen within a few weeks after the United States signed the treaty of Guadalupe Hidalgo, ending the war with Mexico. By this agreement, the government in Washington paid $15,-000,000—the price of the Louisiana Purchase—for territory that became in time the states of California, Nevada, and Utah, and sections of Wyoming, Colorado, Arizona, and New Mexico. If, by the acre, this did not seem to be quite a "noble bargain" on the surface, *underneath* it was, for below the surface was *gold*.

When, in January of 1848, James Wilson Marshall left Sutter's Fort for Coloma Valley, he grumbled no less than other workmen sent off to toil for old Sutter. Jim was expected to build a saw and grist mill on the banks of the American River, and for company was permitted to take along Pete Weimer, his wife and kids—Pete to do the heavy work, his wife the cooking, and the youngsters to get in every-body's way.

Each night, Marshall went to let the water flow through the tailrace of the mill they were building, and the first thing each morning he went, sleepy-eyed and hungry, to shut it off. So the time was about seven-thirty o'clock one morning, when, staring down at the rock in the millrace, Jim Marshall detected the glitter of flecks some six inches beneath the surface of the water.

"I was entirely alone at the time," Jim Marshall said afterward. "I picked up one or two pieces and examined them attentively, and having some general knowledge of minerals, I could not call to mind more than two which in any way resembled this—sulphuret of iron, very bright and brittle; and gold, bright yet malleable. I then tried it between two rocks and found that it could be beaten into a different shape, but not broken."

As to what happened later, there are conflicting stories, but Henry W. Bigler, a Mormon working up in the Coloma Valley, said that Jim Marshall came down from the millrace with his face wreathed in smiles and his old white hat in his arms.

"Boys, by God," Marshall shouted, "I believe I've found a gold mine!"

Bigler said that everyone at the mill gathered round to look at the "samples" Marshall carried in the indented crown of his hat. Wrote the Mormon:

One of our party by the name of Azariah Smith pulled out a five-dollar gold piece and compared the coin with the particles of gold. There was a difference in looks, but this we accounted for on account of the alloy in the coin. None of us had ever seen gold dust before, but we were certain that this was gold.

No one was more certain than Jim Marshall.

"Oh boys, by God," he cried, "it is the pure stuff."

He wrapped his samples in a handkerchief and set off for Sutter's Fort on the quickest journey he ever made. Old Sutter, that ever-cautious German, had to read a long article about gold in the *Encyclopaedia Americana* before he would commit himself. Then Sutter, packing the bottle of whiskey that he always carried when he was in a carefree mood, followed Marshall back to the Coloma Valley.

Everyone knew the truth now: there was gold here, perhaps several fortunes in gold, and the necessity was to keep the discovery to themselves. But knowledge like this never stays secret, as Sutter learned to his sorrow. Soon there was not anybody left at Sutter's Fort to tend the tanning vats or anything else, for they were all down in the Coloma Valley. On March 15, 1848 the news reached San Francisco through an item in a little pioneer newspaper called the *Californian*:

GOLD MINE FOUND. In the newly made raceway of the saw-mill recently erected by Captain Sutter, on the American fork, gold has been found in considerable quantities. One person brought thirty dollars worth to New Helvetia, gathered there in a short time. California, no doubt, is rich in mineral wealth; great chances here for scientific capitalists. Gold has been found in almost every part of the country.

Of course the *Star,* the *Californian's* rival newspaper, branded this story "a sham and superb take-in," for it was a poor pioneer editor who, awakened from a sound sleep, did not say automatically that all other editors were hopeless liars. But within a very short time both newspapers were closed for the same reason: the proprietors had departed for the "gold diggings." For that matter, so had almost everyone else in San Francisco.

The story of Marshall's discovery moved eastward, but few believed it. Congress asked for information and was told by its consul, Thomas O. Larkin, "Gold nuggets weighing sixteen and even twenty-five pounds are being found." Samples to justify this statement reached Washington, along with other stories: of five men on the Feather River who had made $75,000 in three months; of men along the Trinity River who were finding at least $100 in gold every day; of three Frenchmen who pulled up a tree stump and picked $5,000 in gold nuggets from its roots. Not much more was needed.

All at once the rush was on to reach California— and its riches—by any route. Among those caught up in this frenzy was Johnny Nichols of Salem, Massachusetts. Johnny was given a banquet by friends before he left for the diggings, and Johnny, with a poetical bent, offered a parody to be sung to the melody of Stephen Foster's "O Susanna:"

I came from Salem City
With my wash bowl on my knee,
I'm going to California,
The gold dust for to see.
It rained all night the day I left,
The weather it was dry,
The sun so hot I froze to death,
Oh, brothers, don't you cry.

Oh, California,
That's the land for me;
I'm going to Sacramento
With my wash bowl on my knee.

2.

The eight verses of Johnny Nichols's parody, which became known as "The California Immigrant," spoke the spirit of the trickle of gold-seekers to the West that by 1849 swelled into a tidal wave. Whether they came overland, by the long sea route around Cape Horn, or by the so-called shorter, bug-infested way across the Isthmus of Panama, one thing was certain: they all suffered the tortures of the damned. Overland, Indians waited to massacre them; by sea, shysters in New York City waited to sell them, at fabulous prices, outfits they did not need, and to load them up with cases of canned goods that invariably exploded in the first of many wave-tossed storms; across Panama—well, it was better to forget the trip through those sultry jungles, for only a fool ever returned that way.

But by the tens of thousand they came, nonetheless, making of San Francisco a port without an equal in the world. Along swampy avenues that some swore were so muddy a man and mule could sink from sight and that often bore such signs as "This street impassable, not even Jackassable," men in flannel shirts and hip boots rubbed elbows with men in black silk hats and frock coats, and glanced only briefly at Orientals in satin jackets and pantaloons, or at the exotic garb of Malayans, Kanakas, Turks, Chileños. San Francisco Bay became a forest of ships' masts and often vessels were left stranded in the mud as entire crews took off for the gold diggings.

Bayard Taylor, a visiting newspaperman, wrote:

By the tens of thousands they came, making of San Francisco a

The appearance of San Francisco at night, from the water, is unlike anything I ever beheld. The houses are mostly of canvas, which is made transparent by the lamps within, and transform them, in the darkness, to dwellings of solid light. Seated on the slopes of its three hills, the tents pitched among the chaparral to the very summits, it gleams like an amphitheatre of fire. Here and there shines out brilliant points, from the decoy-lamps of the gambling-houses; and through the indistinct murmur of the streets comes by fits the sound of music from their hot and crowded precincts. The picture has in it something unreal and fantastic; it impresses one like the cities of the magic lantern, which a motion of the hand can build or annihilate.

port without an equal. The Bay became a forest of ships' masts

The gaming rooms were always thronged. "Copper-hued Kanakas, Mexicans rolled in their serapes, and Peruvians thrust through their ponchos," Taylor said, "stand shoulder to shoulder with the brown and bearded American miners." The place reeked of bad whiskey. The chink of coins at the monte tables sometimes was broken by the music from the bar. "At the Aguila de Oro," Taylor reported, "there is a full band of Ethiopian serenaders, and at the other hells, violins, guitars, or wheezy accordions." Tobacco smoke added to the stifling heat. A flare-up of temper produced a flash of knives, a bark of pistols. Even the best hotels were mostly gaming rooms and bars. For sleeping quarters the owners provided tiny cubicles, or a dormitory lined with bunk beds. The common hairbrush was chained to a post so that it could not be stolen; the common toothbrush was left free since no one ever was known to carry one away.

If San Francisco seemed an illusion created by a magic lantern, so too did its inhabitants. Within a week, most visitors had departed, striking off for Sacramento, which was the gateway to the northern mines at Marysville, Hangtown, and Nevada City, or for Stockton, the gateway to the southern mines on the Stanislaus and Tuolumne Rivers. With fiddle and deck of cards (the "California prayer book"), the prospector set out with high hopes and stout heart for the diggings, part of a stream of 260,000 fortune-seekers who would pour into the California territory in the twelve years after 1849. In shanty towns that bore such intriguing names as Git-up-and-git, Bogus

Thunder, Shinbone Creek, and Lazy Man's Canyon they staked out their claims, set up their gear, and waited for Lady Luck to kiss their bearded cheeks.

Few women ventured into the gold diggings and the life of the prospector often became desperately lonely. He wrote endless letters to tell the folk back home what a hilarious life he was living, and all the while he sat glumly gazing out the door and wondering if the infernal rain would ever stop. Even though his shack might cost him a king's ransom for rent, with that sort of leaky roof, it rained more inside than out. There were a few "yellow-kivered" novels to read, provided a miner could afford candles at four dollars a pound. Men divided into couples for a Virginia reel, and one sport woke up the camp by breaking the pool cues and finishing a game by shooting the balls into the pockets with his pistol.

Whenever the weather turned fair, there was more than enough work to do. A Forty-Niner's "claim," usually covering an area of forty square feet, could be held for only ten days unless he remained on the spot. As a rule, from four to six miners worked as a company. If they called their stake "Bunker Hill," you could be pretty certain they were Boston boys, and if they named a claim "Illinois," you could be just as certain that they dreamed at night of the rolling prairies.

They worked the surface soil or "top dirt" in a "Long Tom," which was a trough about twenty feet long and eight inches deep. This contraption was made of wood, except for a six-foot section of per-

forated sheet iron, called the "riddle," beneath which
was the "riffle box." Three or four men shoveled the
top dirt into the Long Tom and water washed it
down to the riddle where another man kept the dirt
in motion with a hoe. Since gold was very heavy, it
sank to the bottom and thus passed through the
perforations of the riddle into the riffle box.

Working the top dirt was slow and laborious,
and many miners, anxious to make a fortune in a
hurry, disdained this process. Their plan was to
reach the richer deposits in the bedrock, which meant
"sinking a shaft"—a job not unlike digging a well—
until they struck the bedrock. The task now was to
search for "crevices" containing the ore, and this
work, which was called "drifting coyote holes," con-
sisted of digging passages from the main shaft to
other sections of the bedrock. One of two things could
happen in a coyote hole: with luck you struck a

They worked the surface soil in a Long Tom

crevice, or, more likely, the air grew so impure that it extinguished the headlamps and drove you back to the main shaft.

Some struck it rich, but most did not and were likely to agree with the sad sentiments in one verse of "The Miner's Progress":

> *Thus spake this Pilgrim from the East,*
> *"I am a wretched man,*
> *For lust of gold has lured me to*
> *The shovel and the pan.*
> *I saw in dreams, a pile of gold*
> *Its dazzling radiance pour;*
> *No more my visions are of gold,*
> *Alas! my hopes are* ore."

Yet it was difficult to crush this dream, once it had burned its way like a fever into a prospector's soul. A great many Forty-Niners who cursed Lady Luck for betraying them in California were ready and eager to flirt with the old gal when, in 1858, a new cry rang across the nation: "Pike's Peak or Bust!"

3.

For more than thirty years pioneers, traveling the Santa Fé Trail (see map, page 74), had rolled dustily over the territory that one day would become the state of Colorado. Mountain men had strung their forts through here, Mormons had settled briefly at Pueblo, and Frémont and Kit Carson had crammed official journals with scientific information gathered on their explorations of the region.

Then in 1857 everything went wrong in the East: men were out of jobs; executives complained about businesses no longer making a profit; bankers worried over their deposits. Out of work, Easterners began to move westward in larger numbers, hoping for a turn in fortune.

Very few Easterners, however, striking out for the West, looked upon that part of the Kansas Territory now called Colorado as a logical objective until, on September 4, 1858, a startling headline appeared in the *Kansas Weekly Press:*

> Gold! Gold!! Gold!!! Gold!!!!
> Hard to Get and Heavy to Hold,
> California and Frasers River "no whar!" ...
> Cherry Creek and Pike's Peak Ahead!!!

The story that followed naturally failed to tell that the Cherokee Indians had discovered gold in Colorado eight years before. The important point was that on a day in the late summer of 1858 George Simpson had brought his pan and shovel down to Cherry Creek—near the site of present-day Denver—and had "found the color" in the first panful he washed.

That news was enough—the country went wild with the Colorado gold fever. Over mountain trails, new seekers of quick fortune came, moving the *Hannibal* (Missouri) *Messenger* to comment poetically:

> *Then ho! for the mountains, where the yellow dust is found,*
> *Where the grizzly bear, and buffalo, and antelope abound;*

We'll gather up the dust along the golden creek,
And make our "pile" and start for home. Hurrah
for Pike's Peak!

Although more than an estimated 100,000 entered Colorado during the spring of 1859, it is doubtful if more than a few ever "made their pile" and started for home. Yet these miners dotted the future map of Colorado with new towns: Mount Vernon, Breckinridge, Empire, and the Gold Hills above Cripple Creek that prospectors called a "$30,000,000 cow pasture." Georgetown and Mill City, Boulder and Golden were towns that owed their existence to these glamorous days. Here miners "stocked up" before heading for "the hills." (For location of mining centers mentioned in this chapter, see page 173.)

Afterward, the "Pike's-Peak-or-Busters" who failed had to return home, a fact that wrenched the heart of a reporter for the *Kansas Press* in June of 1859, who "bled" as "mutterings, loud and deep, were heard against those who had humbugged them." Men, returning home, "were swearing like pirates," and the reporter for the *Kansas Press* offered a prediction: "We should not wonder if we heard of terrible outbreaks, [and] when this emigration reaches the river towns, murder and robberies may become common." It was a pitiful scene the reporter for the *Kansas Press* pictured—of foot emigrants, with their hand carts, starving to death—but an equal number were on their way to Nevada where there were strange rumors of a new kind of strike in the Washoe Valley.

That spring a number of miners were working in the streams of Six-Mile Canyon, on property, as they would learn in time, that belonged to "Old Pancake" (Henry) Comstock. There wasn't much water and so the miners dug a hole as a sort of reservoir. When they had gone down about four feet they struck a stratum of "black stuff" filled with spangles of native gold. What they had found was a great bed of sulphuret of silver—the famous Comstock Lode—and when they packed the ore over the Sierras on eighty mules, they learned that it was worth $5,000 a ton.

White bars of silver displayed in a banker's window in San Francisco were enough to start the rush into Nevada. Overnight Virginia City, named for a drunk called "Old Virginny" and perched close to the Comstock Lode, became famous from coast to coast. The stream of prospectors grew from hundreds into thousands and then into tens of thousands. Great mines like the Ophir, Mexican, Central, Gould, and Curry became known around the world as the Comstock Lode yielded more than $300,000,000 in gold and silver in twenty years. The Big Bonanza —a fifty-four-foot-wide section of the lode worth two-thirds of this amount—was struck in 1873.

By now Virginia City was a roaring metropolis of thirty thousand and the home of the *Territorial Enterprise,* the "first newspaper in the howling wilderness of Nevada." Grizzled miners danced in Piper's Opera House on a floor mounted on springs, guzzled in saloons that sprang up like toadstools after a rain, and gathered in the gaming houses where one evening a luckless fellow dropped $38,000 on the flip of a single faro card. No saloon-keeper ever bothered to make change for a five-dollar gold piece.

4.

To explore "the mineral productions of every kind" had been among Jefferson's instructions to Lewis and Clark, but neither they nor the sturdy mountain men who pursued the beaver ever suspected the enormous wealth beneath their feet.

Montana's first gold was discovered in 1852, but a full-fledged rush did not develop until nine years later with the report of a strike on Grasshopper Creek, and a year later, forty-five men were working placers there. Former Confederate soldiers, seeking a new life, clambered into Montana's rocky land, naming it "The Stubtoe State." The veins of silver discovered later at Butte played out after a time, but it was what, in 1880, Marcus Daly found beneath the silver—the future Anaconda Copper Mine—that made Butte "the richest hill in the world."

Gold in the Black Hills of South Dakota sent new hordes streaming into these grayish stretches of ridges and mounds that the Indians considered sacred ground, and set off a bloody Indian war (see Chapter 9). Wherever quick riches beckoned, the prospector grabbed his shovel and pan, mounted his faithful burro, and hit for the hills. Usually when the day ended, he was inclined to agree with those

Chinese miners, who in the early days of the California gold rush, sang:

> *Workee, workee*
> *All same workee,*
> *No time thinkee,*
> *No time see;*
> *Me no likee,*
> *Why fo' workee,*
> *Dampoor ricee,*
> *Dampoor tea.*

6.

"GIT ALONG, LITTLE DOGIE":
The Empire of the Cowboy

The birthplace of the cowboy was in that part of southeast Texas known as the *brasada,* or brush country. As an influence, dominating the history of the wild and woolly West, the cowboy's reign lasted twenty years, or about as long as the reign of the mountain man. Without the Civil War the cowboy could never have emerged as a driving force in shaping a nation, and once the homesteader dug solid roots into the West this cattle-driving, carefree, gun-toting figure had no chance of enduring. Luck made him a romantic character—a great deal of luck.

Few were the western cowboys who realized that the business of driving cattle to market was older than the nation. As early as the 1660's, cattle traders from Boston were moving into the Connecticut River Valley to buy stock that, by various routes, were driven to a point a few miles west of Worcester, where the herds followed a well-beaten course, the Bay State Cow Path.

By the 1800's, there were annual cattle drives by Kentuckians who led their hogs and cows through the Cumberlands and the Blue Ridge Mountains into Tidewater Virginia. Two decades later, farmers from Ohio, Indiana, and Illinois drove cattle eastward over the Three Mountain Trail that entered Pennsylvania near present-day Pittsburgh and then followed a path closely approximating the modern Pennsylvania Turnpike. Thousands of hogs, horses, and Kentucky-bred mules, as well as cattle, were driven over the Tuscarora, Kittatinny, and Blue mountains—by no less than a miracle of perseverance, it would seem today.

If they reached Harrisburg somewhat thinner of carcass, no one should have wondered. The cattle speculator, who really knew his business, shrugged. A day before arriving in market he had his drovers "salt" his cattle; then, by letting them drink their fill of water, several tons were added to the herd's gross weight. This practice, writing the term "watered stock" into the American language, simply revealed that there were tricks in all trades.

The Texas cowboy, of course, embellished the business with frills all his own. No one could ever deny that he was a unique individual. But the Texas cowboy also owed debts to others: first to the Spaniards; then to a war; and finally to the railroad builders.

The long-horned Andalusian cattle that escaped from early Spanish explorers and roamed in wild herds over the Plains were never long on beauty.

Tall and bony, slab-sided and coarse-haired, with horns sometimes spreading more than six feet, and tails dragging on the ground, here were beasts to chill the nerves of any greenhorn. (Indeed, the first shipment of Texas longhorns, reaching New York City in 1854, cleared the streets as mothers clutched their children and stout-hearted men raced for the nearest saloons, not believing what their eyes beheld). Out on the Plains the cowboy could handle these longhorned varmints quite comfortably, and again he was indebted to early explorers for leaving behind the Moorish horse that the Spaniards called *mesteño* and Americans renamed the mustang. Ultimately the cow pony became a mixture of this wild stray and the Kentucky saddle horse, making it as tough as leather and as fast as lightning, and capable of riding to exhaustion anything on four feet.

For a long time, about the best that could be said for the Texas longhorn was that it proved to be a confounded nuisance. As meat, where could you sell it? To the north was a land of savage Indians, and to the east the topography of the country discouraged a profitable cattle drive. The few who tried such drives came back to Texas, admitting that they had been fools. Shipment by sea was out of the question, considering steamship freight rates. True, there was some trade in hides, but that turned out to be a starve-to-death proposition, and so at the time of the Civil War any Texan who depended on longhorns for existence apparently had a head stuffed with loco weed.

The first shipment of Texas longhorns cleared the streets

With large numbers of Texans off fighting for the Confederacy, the wild herds multiplied like the ticks on their legs. Veterans of the struggle between the states came home cussing Lincoln for this unexpected problem, but their grumbling soon ended. The war had changed everything, as Joseph G. McCoy shrewdly guessed.

McCoy was a Northerner out of Illinois who understood how the appetites of Union soldiers for meat had so decreased the North's cattle population that a herd worth from three to five dollars a head in Texas would bring ten times that much in New York City—if you could get the longhorns there. But McCoy also understood that, with the war ended, the railroads once again were pushing westward. "Walk your cattle to the railroad," he said to any livestock man who would listen, an idea that made him the father of the Texas cattle trade.

2.

Joe McCoy was the youngest of three Illinois cattle shippers operating in Springfield and Sangamon County, which had been Lincoln's stamping ground on the way to the presidency, and apparently personal ambition mixed with a sense of national destiny was what the land of Lincoln bred most naturally. There was a lot of Old Abe in Joe: both were tall to the point of gawkiness; both dreamers with the streak of gamblers; both quiet men who, when stirred up, turned into spellbinders.

In 1867, when the Kansas Pacific Railroad reached Abilene, Kansas, and stuck up a plank sign-post for a depot, Joe was not far behind. Abilene at that time Joe described as "a very small, dead place, consisting of about one dozen log huts, low, small rude affairs, four-fifths of which were covered with dirt for roofing; indeed, but one shingle roof could be seen in the city. The business of the burg was conducted in two small rooms, mere log huts, and, of course, the inevitable saloon also in a log hut. . . ."

The name Abilene had come out of the Bible, and perhaps that was a good omen. Joe, a deeply religious man, would have thought so. And Joe, a practical cattle shipper, would quickly have recognized other advantages: the nearby vast unsettled country; the excellent grass; the abundance of water. America's first wide-open rip-roaring, successful cow town could be built here, and Joe McCoy knew it.

There would come a time when Abilene would have three miles of railroad siding and think nothing of shipping three thousand head of cattle a day. Much of the credit for this achievement belonged to McCoy, but not quite all.

A kind word also must be spoken for Jesse Chisholm, whom McCoy called "a semi-civilized Indian" although he was the son of a Scotch father and a Cherokee mother and later the industrious, honest husband of a Creek girl. Jesse was a trader who could speak half a dozen Indian languages, and the Chisholm Trail, which he established, and which has enshrined his name in history, also made Abilene. (See map, page 106.)

By 1869, Texans, coming up from Brownsville, San Antonio, Austin, and Fort Worth, each year were driving north 350,000 head of cattle. Crossing the Red River, they entered the Indian Territory that later became Oklahoma. Lush grass tempted them onward, despite the risks—across the Washita, the Canadian, the Cimarron, the Salt Fork of the Arkansas—and so in time to Abilene.

That was how they began—the first cow town, the first cow trail. As competition quickened, as other railroads fought for business, other trails acquired fame, and the life and death of a cow town depended on friendly or unfriendly freight rates, grass, water. The Shawnee Trail, a bandit's paradise, ran through Fort Worth, with branches to Baxter Springs in Kansas and Sedalia in Missouri. The Western Trail led the longhorns to Dodge City, Kansas, which proudly styled itself "the Cowboy Capital of the World," and eventually to Ogallala in far-off Nebraska. The Goodnight-Loving Trail provided rich summer grass as the herds thundered their way up to Wyoming's Cheyenne. No matter which route a cowboy journeyed, he agreed:

> *You always came in when the fresh meat had*
> *ceased*
> *And the road of the pathway of empire was*
> *greased*
> *By the bacon we fried on the way.*

The first four cattle trails: Chisholm, Shawnee (sometimes called Sedalia), Western, and Good-night Loving (sometimes called Pecos)

3.

Driving a herd of twenty-five hundred longhorns along these trails was no job for a cowboy who did not like a hard life fraught with unanticipated dangers. The narrow-faced animals he drove could be mean-tempered and pugnacious, and anyone who approached a longhorn on foot took his life in his hands, for the devil would charge in an instant. Worst of all were the wild cattle living in the dark forests near the Gulf. They were called "mossy-horned steers" because, it was said, they had existed so long among the trees that moss grew on their horns.

In Texas, where a drive started, the drover's first job was to travel through the cattle country, buying animals where he could, until he had assembled his herd. Next he hired his eight cowboys—men who would be loyal, dependable, and able to cope with any emergency. Then came the labor of finding a man to herd the horses (sometimes two "horse-wranglers" were required) and since each cowboy needed from five to seven horses to ride each day on the trail, as many as a hundred horses were purchased. The chuck wagon was an item to buy with a knowing eye, for it became the headquarters of the outfit, carrying the water, cooking utensils, thirty days' provisions, the few personal belongings of the crew, the trail boss's papers, and all sleeping equipment. The hiring of the cook completed the outfit, and although the cook was called the "old woman," his hard face, profane language, and the notch or two on his gun reminded the cowboy to smile when he used this flippant form of address.

Around the Gulf of Mexico, a cattle drive might begin as early as March 1 and on the Panhandle as late as October 1. For the first few days the restlessness of the herd kept the outfit riding day and night. Not until the cattle were off their accustomed range, where there was always the risk of a stampede to regular feeding grounds, could the drover breathe easily. At first the herd might be driven twenty-five or thirty miles a day in an effort to break the longhorns by tiring them out so that they would rest at night instead of running over the country. By the time the herd was ready to leave Texas, the drive slowed down to the usual pace—ten to fifteen miles a day. The last town of any size in Texas was where the thirty days' supplies were bought since the outfit would not see another store until it reached Kansas.

When breakfast was ready, the cook roused the sleeping cowboys and the day's work started. Jokes about the "old woman's" fare might be commonplace, but there was a sound reason why the cook's wages ran higher than those of top hands among the riders. If the cook knew his job, he was the jewel of the outfit. You could tell the cook's value by his sourdough biscuits: if they were delicious, the cook was a gem, and if they made you gag, the scamp should be lynched on reaching Abilene. Coffee was another test. Any good trail cook knew that coffee too strong didn't exist—only weak people.

The herd, on the move, would stretch out for a mile

If the three meals of the day followed much the same pattern, the cowboy grinned and said nothing, accepting the rule of the range that "only a fool argues with a woman, a mule, or the cook," although in private you might find him humming:

Oh, it's bacon and beans most every day,
I'd as soon be a-eatin' prairie hay.

The cowboys caught their horses for the morning drive. The herd, on the move, would stretch out for a mile, an inspiring sight. The two oldest riders, in the lead, "pointed herd" (that is, directed it). About one third of the way back came the swing riders; another third back the flank riders; and at the rear three riders "brought up the drag." These were the fellows who kept the slow, lazy, or lame longhorns toiling onward, and by the time the day ended these riders sometimes became almost as cantankerous as the cattle they had been cussing since sun-up.

All night two hands, riding in opposite directions, circled the herd. At the first sign of restlessness the men began to sing, for the sound of their voices quieted the animals, and especially on stormy nights did the cowboy need to be in good voice. His comrades, sleeping, had their night horses saddled and bridled and often clutched reins in hand, ready to spring into action at the first sound of trouble.

Stampedes had a wide variety of causes: the howl of coyotes; the presence of buffalo; the striking of a match to light a pipe; a pony shaking his saddle; the snap of a broken stick. The rainy season, with its flashes of lightning, its claps of thunder, posed other terrors. Thirst was still another worry. If the cattle had to go too long without water, almost anything could happen. Andy Adams, one of the greatest of Texas cattlemen, remembered such an occasion:

Good cloudy weather would have saved us, but in its stead was a sultry morning without a breath of air, which bespoke another day of sizzling heat. We had not been on the trail over two hours before the heat became almost unbearable to man and beast. Had it not been for the condition of the herd, all might yet have gone well; but over three days had now elapsed without water for the cattle, and they became feverish and ungovernable. The lead cattle turned back several times, wandering aimlessly in any direction, and it was with considerable difficulty that the herd could be held on the trail. The rear overtook the lead, and the cattle gradually lost all semblance of a trail herd. Our horses were fresh, however, and after about two hours' work, we once more got the herd strung out in trailing fashion; but before a mile had been covered, the leaders again turned, and the cattle congregated into a mass of unmanageable animals, milling and lowing in their fever and thirst. The milling only intensified their sufferings from the heat, and the outfit split and quartered them again and again, in the hope that this unfortunate outbreak might be checked. No sooner was the milling stopped than they would surge hither and yon, sometimes half a mile, as ungovernable as the waves of an ocean. After wasting several hours in this manner, they finally turned back over the trail, and the utmost effort of every man in the outfit failed to check them. We threw our ropes in their faces, and when this failed, we resorted to shooting; but in defiance of the fusillade and the smoke they walked sullenly through the line of horsemen across their front. Sixshooters were discharged so close to the leaders' faces as to singe their hair; yet under a noonday sun they disregarded this and every other device to turn them and passed wholly out of our control. In a number of instances wild steers deliberately walked against our horses, and then for the first time a fact dawned on us that chilled the marrow in our bones—*the herd was going blind.*

Andy Adams looked down upon the trail—the bones of men and animals were bleaching there— and he knew that this was not the first time such a tragedy had struck. The foreman recognized the only possible solution: the herd must be driven to Indian Lakes. He said:

The herd will travel day and night, and instinct can be depended on to carry them to the only water they know.

Andy thought: "It was no vague statement of

the man who said that if he owned hell and Texas,
he'd rent Texas and live in hell, for if this isn't Billy
hell, I'd like to know what you call it."

Andy and his friends started back for Indian
Lakes. He described the scene there next day when,
at noon:

> . . . the cattle began to arrive at the water holes
> in squads of from twenty to fifty. Pitiful objects as
> they were, it was a novelty to see them reach the
> water and slack their thirst. Wading out into the
> lakes until their sides were half covered, they would
> stand and low in a soft moaning voice, often for half
> an hour before attempting to drink. Contrary to our
> expectation, they drank very little at first, but stood
> in the water for hours. After coming out, they would
> lie down and rest for hours longer and then drink
> again before attempting to graze, their thirst over-
> powering hunger. That they were blind there was
> no question, but with the causes that produced it
> once removed, it was probable their eyesight would
> gradually return.

A cattleman like Andy Adams learned in time to
know his business like the palm of his hand. He
learned how to handle longhorns. Riding on the
prairies during a lightning storm, sometimes he
watched balls of fire play around the cattle's horns
and the horses' ears, and knew that his was a risky
business. Perhaps that was why he loved it.

4.

But there were also man-made dangers. For
example, wherever Texas longhorns traveled they
were likely to become involved in the "Fever War"

and it would be years before anyone would realize that appointing inspectors to examine these Texas cattle and to sort out the sick was not going to do much good. In time, experts from the United States Department of Animal Husbandry discovered why domestic cattle were likely to be stricken after the Texas herds passed through—the Texas longhorn carried a tick against which it was immune, but this little rascal, dropping off the leg of a longhorn, needed only to crawl onto a domestic cow and lay its eggs to leave destruction behind. Without this knowledge, Missourians often turned back Texas cattlemen—and turned them back at the point of six-shooters, if necessary.

Another man-made danger was the Indian. With good reason, an old time Texas "waddy" or cowboy like James H. Cook would recall that, strangely, "a white man's horse was generally afraid of the sight or scent of an Indian, just as Indian ponies were afraid of a white man." Cook was certain that when the horses of Texans scented Indians "they sniffed the air, snorted, ran together, and showed terror by their looks and actions."

Cook at least hoped this belief was well founded when, traveling northward from Texas on his first cattle drive, he crossed the Llano River into Indian territory. Old-timers told Cook to be careful, especially of the hours "during the early part of each evening and also just at the break of day," since these were "the Indian's favorite times for deviltry." As later events proved, Cook had not been misled.

Across the Llano, the rough, broken country was dominated by large cedar thickets. Cook looked at those brakes and thought: "The Indians could slip up close and kill me with an arrow."

An old-timer told him to relax. "They cannot run their horses in that brake," he said.

Cook didn't relax, but he discovered that the old-timer knew whereof he spoke.

It was chilly that night when the outfit camped —a huge fire of dry wood lighted up every face— and Cook, riding back to camp with rifle in hand, had just touched his foot to the ground when he heard shots—two dozen in quick succession, he said, which was placing a high trust in a precise memory. Anyhow, firing a shot in response, Cook recalled:

. . . My horse had also turned his head when the shots were fired. A bullet struck him in the forehead, and he went down at my feet. I jumped away from that campfire as quickly as possible and crawled under a big cedar tree, the branches of which came close to the ground. The next moment most of the horse herd came tearing right through camp. We had ropes stretched from the wagon wheels to some trees to make a corral in which to catch the horses, and the horses ran against the ropes, upsetting the wagon.

Every man in camp ran for his life into the thicket. The horses which were tied about near camp, all saddled, ran on their ropes and broke them and decamped with the other animals—all save one horse. Some Indian had slipped into camp before the firing started, cut the picket-rope of this horse, and led him away.

The horses ran into the cattle herd, and away

went the cattle into a big cedar brake containing many old dead trees. There was a smashing and crashing and about as great an uproar as any cowboy ever heard. The men with the cattle did not dare yell at the animals or sing to them, lest Indians locate and slip an arrow into somebody.

I lay quite still under the tree. After a time I heard Roberts's [the foreman's] voice calling out: "Don't let 'em get away with the horses, boys! Stay with 'em! Come on, boys, where are you?" I do not know where Roberts disappeared to when the horses stampeded through camp, but he certainly went somewhere—for a few minutes. I don't see, either, how he expected us to hold that horse herd. One by one I could hear the boys answer him. I did not like to get out from beneath that tree, but I did not care to be called a coward, so I joined him, although I thought it the most foolish thing we could possibly do. It was so dark that an Indian could slip up within three feet of a man and not be seen.

Investigation in the clear, reassuring daylight disclosed that the outfit had not suffered very badly:

. . . The horse herd had scattered in every direction after passing camp. Some ran into the cattle herd, where they were held by the boys with the herd, and one bunch of horses were chased up a cañon by the Indians for some distance. The horses were unable to get out of it because of the perpendicular bluffs, and the Indians were afraid to drive them back down the cañon, so they had to let the animals go. As it was, the savages got away with about a fourth of our horses.

Trouble with the Indians took many forms. In Oklahoma Territory, where the Cherokees and

Creeks were called the "civilized tribes," the Indians reflected their higher culture by demanding toll from Texans for the privilege of driving the herds through their lands. The payment of course was made in cattle, but a drover cussed under his breath as he watched part of his cows driven off (to a cattleman any bovine was a "cow" and females were called "she stuff").

Near the Missouri–Kansas line a new menace was the appearance of the bandit-guerrillas who had fought under the notorious Quantrill during the Civil War. These "hijackers" also demanded toll for permitting the herd to pass on, and a Texas outfit, outnumbered ten to one by these border ruffians, could only stand aside as another fifty or hundred cows were cut from the herd.

Yet, despite every hazard, the cowboy, proud and tough, stuck to his job and, during the period from 1867 to 1884, probably more than 5,000,000 Texas longhorns followed the trails northward to Abilene and Dodge City and to other shipping points in Montana, Nebraska, and Wyoming. When the herd reached town it was assigned grazing space where it could fatten up while the owner awaited a favorable selling price. Meanwhile the cowboy, paid his wages for the drive, was ready for his "fun." Somewhat skittishly would the Topeka *Commonwealth* report in July of 1868: "At this writing, Hell is now in session in Abilene."

It certainly was.

7.

GOOD GUYS AND BAD GUYS:
And Some Gals, Too

Joe McCoy, with his deeply religious streak, must have shuddered at what he had created in Abilene. In its boom days, as many as a thousand Texans invaded the town at the same time. A trip to the barbershop for a bath, shave, and haircut—and perhaps to have his mustache blackened and "set"— prepared the cowboy for his fling. A correspondent for the New York *Tribune,* visiting the place, could hardly credit what his eyes beheld:

> Gathered together in Abilene and its environs is the greatest collection of Texas cowboys, rascals, desperados, and adventuresses the United States has ever known. There is no law, no restraint in this seething cauldron of vice and depravity.

To anyone who walked Texas Street during Abilene's heyday, the report did not seem a gross exaggeration. Saloons, dance halls, gambling dens were thicker than the lice on the hogs rooting in the gutters. Perfumed "ladies" left a scented trail as they walked by in their tasseled white kid half-boots, and the paint on their faces may have explained why no paint remained for the bare clapboards of the buildings.

The two blocks of Texas Street were never without bands of drunken cowboys. At any moment the arrival of a new outfit might be announced by the pound of ponies, the exuberant firing into the air of six-shooters, the wild yell of men who knew Abilene as a "wide-open settlement" where there was "no jail, no court" and where "everybody [was] free to be drunk anywhere, to gamble in public, to shoot to kill."

What law existed went by the dubious title of "saloon law"—that is, rules that the proprietors of the dens of vice chose to enforce for the protection of their own seedy enterprises. This "law" respected the cowboy's code, which, as one authority of the period has observed, "held fist-fighting to be a cut beneath them, something reserved for teamsters, bullwhackers, and soldiers." Shooting was different, or administering a pistol whipping, and if these were not possible when facing an opponent, then "wrenching a leg off a chair and clubbing him unconscious," became acceptable.

To appeal to the Texans, there were so many saloons and dance halls named the "Lone Star" scattered across the cow towns of the West that one could not be remembered from another. There really was not any difference among them: almost all served bad whiskey; almost all ran crooked gambling games; almost all supplied a kind of music, ground out on a dilapidated organ or banged out by a weary band, that would have shattered the eardrums of a deaf mute.

The lonesome cowboy, with money in his pockets, was shamefully played for a sucker, but when he lost the last of his bankroll at five-cent chuck-a-luck, more often than not he simply shrugged as though to say: "What's the sense of cartin' the money back to Texas, anyhow?"

John Wesley Hardin, the Texas killer who, at the age of fifteen, shot his first victim and claimed that he added another forty notches to his gun in ensuing years, insisted: "I have seen fast towns, but Abilene beat them all." The statement was about as reliable as Hardin himself—the truth was that Abilene was no worse than most boom towns that flourished during the cowboy's years of influence in the wild and woolly West. Dodge City, for example, became known as "the Gomorrah of the Plains" and enriched the American vocabulary with such terms as "stiff," for a corpse, and "Boot Hill" (a cemetery for those who died with their boots on).

As one cow town gave way to another in popularity, the same gamblers, pickpockets, vice lords, confidence men, and painted women appeared, along with the "bad man" who was far from the romantic figure fiction and the motion pictures sometimes made him. William H. (Billy the Kid) Bonney, Sam Bass, Little Harpe, and Johnny Ringo, to mention

only a few of these celebrated thieves and gun sling-
ers, led mean and narrow lives filled with dirt, pov-
erty, and fear, for there was no real courage in these
rascals. And in time law won out, even in the Abilene
that John Wesley Hardin believed was such a jolly,
rip-roaring town for those with nervous trigger-
fingers.

2.

Despite the claim of Wild Bill Hickok that he
tamed Abilene, the credit for this accomplishment
belonged to the relatively unknown Tom Smith. In
the little town of Kit Carson, Colorado (what town
in the Old West could have a more appropriate
name?) Tom heard that wild and woolly Abilene
was seeking a marshal. Always a quiet chap who
acted according to opportunity, Tom mounted his
big gray horse, Silverheels, and rode into Abilene
in search of the mayor.

"I'm your new marshal," Tom said, believing in
coming to the point.

Mayor Henry looked at a "broad-shouldered,
athletic man about five-feet-eleven inches in height,
who tipped the scales at 170 pounds, stood erect, had
grayish-blue eyes, auburn hair and light mustache."
It was difficult to make Tom speak about himself
and, almost grudgingly, he admitted that his full
name was Thomas James Smith and that he had
been born of Irish parents in New York City in
1840.

"He was fairly well educated, reared a Catholic, and was clean of speech," Mayor Henry remembered. "I never heard him utter a profane word or employ a vulgar phrase. He neither gambled, drank, nor was in the least dissolute otherwise."

"You think you can control the town?" the mayor asked on their first meeting.

"That's what I'm here for, Mr. Henry," Tom Smith answered. "I believe I can control it."

Tom Smith was no dandy, strutting the streets of Abilene. He patrolled the town on horseback, carrying a brace of pistols in shoulder holsters that he kept out of sight, for Tom Smith did not believe in gunplay. He expected to maintain order with his own two fists, an innovation that reputedly set one Texan to moaning: "We don't know no more about fist fightin' than a hog knows about a sidesaddle."

Tom's reply, in the low tone for which he became famous, was that the Texan had better behave himself or learn something about "fist fightin'." Signs appeared in Abilene, prohibiting the carrying of guns. For a time cowpunchers made sport of pulling the signs down, until Tom caught one in the act. The marshal yanked the offender from his pony and gave him a clip on the chin that left the fellow sleeping blissfully until he awakened in the town pokey.

Racks went up in stores, in hotels, in saloons where the cowboys were to park their guns until they left town—and Tom saw that the racks were used. There was the case of Wyoming Frank, who swore no marshal was going to take away his gun.

Tom stalked into the saloon after the tough and there they stood—Wyoming Frank armed with his gun and Tom Smith with his fists. The marshal was quick, and the affair was over before Wyoming Frank quite knew what happened—except that his gun was gone and his head was split wide open.

A few nights later there was gunplay in the Old Fruit Saloon, one of Abilene's worst hangouts. The doors swung open and in walked Tom. The cowboys lined up in a hostile row against the bar. This time Tom whipped out a pistol, but it was a few swipes of his fists that settled the argument. When Tom left the Old Fruit he was carrying a basketful of guns. The town officials raised his salary.

3.

So that was how law came to Abilene, for all that Wild Bill Hickok claimed it was his blazing guns that caused the town to heel. Wild Bill was the dead opposite of Tom, his predecessor in office. Wild Bill was a strutter in his Prince Albert coat and fancy vest, a hard drinker, an incurable poker player, and a gun slinger who boasted that he had killed fifty men before reaching Abilene and that in order to bring peace to the town he was forced to kill a dozen more. (Actually he shot two.) To know the truth about Wild Bill you had to forget his own tales or the romances of the dime novelists and see him through the eyes of the one person who understood him thoroughly, the immortal Calamity Jane.

Old Calam's real name was Martha Jane Canary. Born May 1, 1852 in Princeton, Missouri, she grew up as a robust, dark-eyed, big-boned girl with coarse auburn hair who loved to roam the pine forests near her home. Later when the family moved to Kirkwood, where her father was a preacher, trouble developed with the schoolteacher, who came after her with a ruler, and Calamity Jane scampered home before he could catch her, declaring that she would not study under such a man.

Her father agreed—he had been looking all along for an excuse to settle his family among the Mormons in Salt Lake City—and so the family packed up for the long journey over the trail to Utah. The trip suited Calamity Jane: she could ride a horse and shoot a gun as well as any man and she hadn't an ounce of fear in her for the wild country through which they journeyed. Indeed, when the caravan was surrounded by Indians one night, it was Calamity Jane who rode through the darkness to summon relief from the nearest army post. The rigors of the trip, however, proved more than her father and mother could endure, and the girl reached Salt Lake City an orphan.

Calamity Jane was now thirteen and ready to strike off on her own. Her first job, as a dance-hall girl in Helena, lasted about an hour—life in this kind of "hog ranch" was not for her. But Calam' was adaptable and willing to try anything: dishwashing at Fort Bridger; working with a railroad construction gang (which she managed by dressing like a man); scouting for the army. She loved independence, an outdoor life, the touch of the wind in her hair when she was riding her beloved horse, Bess.

Her first meeting with James Butler Hickok was at an army barracks near Laramie and, for Calamity Jane, gazing upon the already notorious Wild Bill in his store-new leather chaps and wide sombrero, it was a matter of love at first sight. Calam' must have had her good points, for in time she and Wild Bill were secretly married.

The Wild Bill of legend, however, was not the moody, unpredictable, unreliable Wild Bill his wife came to know. She was with Wild Bill in Abilene during the nine months he held office as marshal. In character, Wild Bill's idea of law—he was surely no Tom Smith—was to be judge, jury, and executioner, ruling by his reputation as the "Prince of Pistoleers." One night he gunned down Phil Coe, who was shadowing him because of an old personal feud. Then mistaking a man running toward him for a confederate of Coe's, he also shot him. The second man was Mike Williams, a friend who had been hastening to Wild Bill's assistance. Abilene's citizens organized against their own marshal, forcing him to resign.

Next Calamity Jane waited patiently while Wild Bill went East to win fame and fortune in a Wild West show, but he was soon back for a variety of reasons, one of which was a street brawl he fell into with a group of New York cabbies.

Later still, after Calamity Jane had given birth to a child in a wilderness cave, Wild Bill deserted her, leaving her without food or water, which should have taught her the full measure of the man. But old Calam' simply lost herself in drink and drifting —she forgave him for everything—and they were together in Deadwood, South Dakota, when Wild Bill's career ended with a shot in the back during a poker game.

For those who prefer myth to truth, there may be something romantic in the thought of Wild Bill and old Calam' resting in peace in the same boot hill cemetery in Deadwood, but except for a very few like Tom Smith, who are almost unremembered, the gun-totin' cow town marshals were scarcely unblemished heroes in the wild and woolly West. More often, like Wild Bill, they were known killers who were given their jobs because they were quick on the draw. Certainly the best that could be said for Wyatt Earp, who cleaned up Tombstone, Arizona (and claimed to have cleaned up a great deal more that he didn't) was the fact that he made his gun slinging respectable. Bat Masterson, the marshal of Dodge City, perhaps deserved a better rating, but Bat also was a once-too-willing gun slinger.

Others could be named: for example, King Fisher of Uvalde County, Texas, who once led a band of outlaws and posted a sign: "This is King Fisher's Road. Take the Other." Neither the bad man, nor the town marshal, nor the cowboy—making the long drive from Texas to the railheads in the North—

would write the final chapter in the story of the "cattle kingdom" that by 1876 spread over western Texas, Oklahoma, Kansas, Nebraska, Montana, the Dakotas, Colorado, parts of Utah, Nevada, and New Mexico.

The true hero of this story would be free grass.

4.

Western ranching became the inevitable outgrowth of the cattle drives. The call of the open range was answered by cowboys, scouts, hunters, army men, freighters, and prospectors who had grown weary of toiling with pan and shovel. Good Texas cattle could be bought for from five to ten dollars a head, fattened, and shipped to markets, bringing from thirty-five to fifty dollars.

In the seventies and eighties, before wells were dug to supply the stock, the first consideration in establishing a ranch was water holes and springs. Possession of a water hole meant, generally, that a man controlled the surrounding grassland for a distance of six or seven miles, giving rise to the rule that it was "unneighborly" to start a ranch within fifteen miles of one already in operation. Coulees or valleys offering the cattle protection against blizzards and severe storms were another important consideration in selecting the ranch site.

The cow camp, or first headquarters of the ranch, seldom offered little more than primitive comfort: a pole table; hammock-like beds made of rawhide;

cupboards under the bunks; pegs for hanging up fire-arms; a fireplace, a broom.

As the women arrived in the range lands, the more permanent ranch house began to appear, although that, too, often was quite primitive, consisting of logs or sod covered with hay and earth. In the early migrations women and children, of course, had gone with the men in the trains of "prairie schooners" settling the wild and woolly West; but in the range lands the owners and their cowboys usually staked out their "claims" before the women followed by stagecoach or train.

In either case, the women brought stability, a sense of community to the West. Resourceful, ingenious, they found that they had many roles to play. In many areas they were the only "doctors" who existed, administering to the sick, delivering babies, even though they journeyed many miles to do so. What did these settlers do when they felt ill? "We took a tea made of wild cherry and dogwood bark and rested a while," one pioneer ranch woman wrote, and doubtless for the ailing the rest did achieve great beneficial effect.

More to the point, perhaps, was the fact that the quality of food improved under the presence of the women—diets were better and there was less tendency, as said a settler in the Pacific Northwest, who had previously lived almost exclusively on clams, for his stomach to rise and fall with the tides. Salads made of green shoots began to appear on tables—the women tried to bring a sense of adventure into frontier eating. They brought also a need of education for their children: the schoolhouse, the church, under their driving force, outranked the saloon and jail in importance. Men, moving into the rangeland, sought "empires," but the women built homes, communities, and soon the ranch acquired barnyard, horse paddock, cattle corral, blacksmith shop—became, in short, a place in which to live.

From year to year, as increasing numbers of ranches dotted the western plains, a new form of American life was emerging. Hard though that life proved during its early days, it developed its own customs and traditions. Ranchmen visited in hospitable spirit during the winter months, calling the habit "riding the grub line." Local gossip was eagerly exchanged, and cow-town vices winked at.

The cowboy's existence in the "dog house"—the popular name for the bunkhouse—often was drab during these winter months. He played checkers and dominoes, held stag-dances to kill long winter evenings, joined Lonely Heart Clubs so he would have female companions with whom to correspond, and shot at flies crawling on the ceiling. The cowboy was no fancy critter at home—he would not wear spectacles, considering them a sign of weakness; nor would he be caught in a nightshirt. Such frills were for tenderfeet—the cowboy simply removed coat, hat, boots, and spurs and was ready for bed.

Spring meant hunting for the horses that had been running wild for months and probably needed to be rebroken. All the dreary chores that filled the cowboy's days thereafter—gardening, irrigating meadows, gathering hay—were tolerable because he dreamed of the highlight of his year, the summer round-up. There was always a race then to see who could be first on his horse. Each hand received his orders "for the circle"; then away he sped with a group of four or five comrades to cover the section of the range assigned to him.

Thus, by "combing the country," the strays were found. "Cutting out" came next—the most exciting part of the round-up for, in locating cows of a particular brand, a man had to know how to ride. This was work for the "top hands" and they picked no bones over that fact.

Chow time found the cowboys ready for their favorite foods—mulligan stew, spotted-dog pudding, sourdough biscuits, black coffee you could walk on—and the conversation ran to how far the foreman had "covered his dog," which was the expression for gathering all the cattle in an assigned region. Rest came afterward; then the branding of the calves. In time the rodeo—from the Spanish term for round-up, *el rodeo*—would become an integral part of ranch life, but in the early years the round-up was entirely the "show" of the professional cowboy doing well the job for which he was paid.

5.

In addition to the seasoned cattleman and cowboy, the call of the range appealed unexpectedly to many others. Among the several women, or "cattle

The round-up was entirely the show of the professional cowboy

queens," who operated ranches was Mrs. Bishop Hiff Warren, who, it was said, acquired assets of $10,000,000 and became the wealthiest woman in Colorado.

Another unusual personality stepped off the train at Little Missouri, in the Dakota Bad Lands, at three o'clock of a cool September morning in 1882. He was a slender young man, not very tall and wearing a trim mustache, but what marked him at once was his spectacles. "Four Eyes," the natives called him, contemptuous of a near-sighted tenderfoot above all others. But one day the young man, badgered by a bully in a saloon, laid out the fellow with two well-placed punches, and his nickname was changed to a respectful "Old Four Eyes." Thus did Teddy Roosevelt exhibit the vigor and spirit that eventually made him President of the United States, and made him, in the middle 1880's, one of the most popular ranchers in the Bad Lands. A ballad of the region showed understanding of the forces that drew men to the range:

> *Some came for lungs, and some for jobs,*
> *And some for booze at Big-mouth Bob's;*
> *Some to punch cattle, some to shoot,*
> *Some for vision, some for loot;*
> *Some for views and some for vice,*
> *Some for faro, some for dice;*
> *Some for the joy of a galloping hoof,*
> *Some for the prairie's spacious roof,*
> *Some to forget a face, a fan,*
> *Some to plumb the heart of man;*
> *Some to preach and some to blow,*

Some to grab and some to grow,
Some in anger, some in pride,
Some to taste, before they died,
Life served hot and a la cartee—
And some to dodge a necktie-party.

The rustlers were no myth. They were there, all right, carrying small iron rods on their saddles and changing a brand whenever they could. An L or E could easily be turned into a B and in such fashion the rustler "ran" a brand. Others killed the cattle, buried the hides, and sold the meat in mining camp or town. Up in Wyoming, in the spring of 1892, hard feeling between the rustlers and the cattlemen erupted into a vicious struggle known as the Johnson County War.

6.

Really to understand what happened one had to go back to 1879 when cattlemen, nesters (homesteaders), miners, and freighters founded the town of Buffalo. The nesters(who were farmers) and the cattlemen were at odds from the start, both believing they were right—the farmers putting up fences to protect their crops, and the cattlemen wanting the fences torn down so that their herds could range freely as storms and grass and water supplies necessitated.

The nester, his back up, joined forces with the rustler to break the dominance of the cattleman. That was how the trouble started, and certainly the situation was not improved by the bitter winter of 1886-87 that killed many herds, drove some ranchers out of business, and left jobless cowboys to swell the ranks of the rustlers. South of the Platte, the town of Buffalo became "the rustlers' capital."

One account of the situation reported: "Settlers and cattlemen watched each other cautiously, when they met on Buffalo's boardwalks. They varied their routes to town and pulled shades carefully at night. Some who neglected these precautions were found later, hanging from a cottonwood or shot in the back. Tensions mounted steadily."

Cattlemen, organizing protective associations in Wyoming, had passed legislation that set definite dates for all round-ups when brand inspectors, appointed by the state, could oversee the marking of cattle. In the spring of 1892, however, Johnson County's nesters and small ranchers decided to hold a round-up earlier than the prescribed dates, and the explosion followed. Grim-faced big cattlemen banded together into a society known as the Regulators whose purpose could not be doubted when hired gunmen were imported from Texas, Idaho, and Colorado. A former army officer was placed in command. Fifty-two heavily armed Regulators left on the night of April 5 on a special train for Casper, whence they expected to make a swift march to Buffalo. The town was to be seized, the rustlers captured (or shot, or treated to a necktie party, since such distinctions were purely technical).

When news of this movement reached Buffalo,

the residents would not believe that the cattlemen were serious. Meanwhile the Regulators pulled into Casper. Wagons were waiting for them. So, too, were spies who reported that two of the leaders they most wanted, Nate Champion and Nick Ray, were at the K C ranch, fifty miles south of Buffalo. Cutting the telegraph wires to Buffalo and Sheridan, the Regulators finished the grisly business of killing Champion and Ray. Then they marched northward.

Buffalo at last was willing to believe the worst. The town could not resist the sight of Robert Foote, its leading merchant, galloping from house to house with his black cape and long white beard flapping in the breeze. Foote threw open his store, issuing free guns, ammunition, and tobacco. Sheriff Red Angus swore in one hundred deputies; then started for the K C ranch. A Home Defenders corps of several hundred rushed to the defense of Buffalo. Churches and schoolhouses were turned into barracks.

Warned of these preparations, the cattlemen retreated to the T A ranch, fourteen miles south of Buffalo. The Regulators dug rifle pits and threw up breastworks, but in their haste lost their supply wagons to the Johnson County men, now some four hundred strong. Angus and his boys, preparing to storm the ranch, waited until dark to dig rifle pits within gunshot of the house. A novel device was a "go-devil" or portable barricade of logs, mounted on the running gears of the captured wagons, from which they intended to toss dynamite into the cattlemen's barricade.

Robert Foote galloped from house to house, his black cape and long white beard flapping in the breeze

Forty men were moving the "go-devil" into range when three troops of cavalry from Fort McKinney, under Colonel J. J. Van Horn, came crashing down with bugles blowing. For once that old cliché, "just in the nick of time," seemed entirely appropriate—most of all to the cattlemen, who surrendered to Van Horn. They were held in Cheyenne until Johnson County no longer could meet the cost of their imprisonment, when they were dismissed. Meanwhile soldiers patrolled the streets of Buffalo until tempers cooled.

The "peaceful" ending of the Johnson County War, the most dramatic of all the struggles between cattlemen and rustler-nesters, more or less closed a chapter in the history of the Old West. Struggles with the "woollies" continued longer, however.

7.

Again it was the Spaniards, bringing their silky-fleeced merinos from Castile, who were responsible for the vast sheep herds that eventually roamed the ranges of Colorado, Wyoming, and Montana. Like the cattleman, the sheepherder needed free grazing land if he was to prosper, but there his resemblance with the cowman ended. A sheep flock ate the grass right down to the roots. It was no wonder the ranchers shuddered at the sight of the "woollies."

But the flockmasters kept crossing the range nonetheless. A grazing flock, known as a "band," contained from fifteen hundred to three thousand animals, and could be tended by two men and their dogs.

By the turn of the twentieth century, a familiar sight on the western slopes was the rolling home, or sheep wagon, of these lonely, determined wanderers. This apparatus was no more than a common farm wagon with rounded top and covered sides of canvas where the herders lived in any degree of temperature. Stove, bunks, table, dish cupboard were standard equipment of the living quarters within. So also were the old black coffee pot, the skillet, the Dutch oven.

Angry cattlemen fought the "woollies" almost as fiercely as they fought the rustlers—and fought them none too honorably at times as they organized into raiding bands of "gunnysackers." These raiders—so named because they disguised themselves by wearing gunny-sacks over their heads—attempted to terrorize the sheepmen out of the country. A favorite trick was to destroy a grazing flock by "rimrocking" it (that is, by driving it over cliffs with shouts and curses). Flockmasters were shot or hung. In ten years of the "sheep war" in Wyoming, as many as fifty herders may have been killed and twenty-five thousand sheep destroyed. But the sheep industry would not be driven out of Wyoming by fear and, in time, displaced the cattle industry, only to lose out itself to the persistent onward march of the homesteader and the dry farmer.

But change was the most predictable characteristic of the wild and woolly West—a fact that no one knew better than the greatest of all its showmen, Buffalo Bill. His time on the Plains stretched from the Pony Express to the Iron Horse and saw the Indian become the vanishing American. Great legends were written about Buffalo Bill. The truth was equally exciting.

8.

THE DOMAIN OF BUFFALO BILL:
From Pony Express to Iron Horse

Buffalo Bill's real name was William Frederick Cody. Le Claire in Scott County, Iowa, where Will Cody howled his way into the world on February 26, 1846, was first settled by Anton Le Clair, a celebrated half-breed Indian scholar and interpreter. The death of a son, who was crushed by a rearing horse, so saddened the Cody family that they decided to leave Iowa and so, at the age of six, young Will rode on a thirty-day journey into the Kansas Territory.

Astride a pony, the lad pretended that he was an Indian scout and believed his was the best sport ever. Kansas, soon to bleed in a struggle over whether the territory should be admitted to the Union as a free or slave state, was a tempestuous place in the years from 1854 to 1856—especially for Isaac Cody, Will's father, who held strong views against slavery.

"I was one of the pioneers of the state of Iowa, aided its settlement, helped organize it as a state,"

Isaac told a crowd of hecklers one day. "I voted it should be a *white* state, that Negroes whether slave or free should never be allowed to locate within its limits. I say to you now, and I say it boldly, I propose to exert all my power in making Kansas the same kind of state."

Rabid pro-slavery border ruffians had heard enough. "You black Abolitionist!" they howled. One stabbed Isaac in the back with a bowie knife.

Thereafter, Will understood, Isaac Cody must become a hunted man in Kansas. His father had begun to build a sawmill in Grasshopper Falls, when Will learned that an angry mob had set out to kill him. Will, mounting his pony, remembered forever those moments when he rode onto a group of his father's enemies:

> As I galloped past one of them yelled, "There's Cody's kid now on his way to warn his father. Stop, you, and tell us where your old man is!"
>
> A pistol shot, to terrify me into obedience, accompanied the command. I may have been terrified, but it was not into obedience. I got out of there like a shot, and though they rode hard on my trail my pony was too fast for them. My warning was in time.

Young Will Cody would need this sort of pluck in the months that followed, for pro-slavery mobs constantly hunted his father. Though Isaac eluded them all, his death after a long illness in 1857, Will always believed, resulted from the knife wound he had suffered three years before.

Now the boy found himself the chief support of

his family. A leggy youngster, with fearless brown eyes and unruly blond hair, he was respected even then as a good rider and a deadly shot. In Kansas he had seen more than forty thousand pioneers in their prairie schooners cussing the mud as they pushed their way westward toward California and the Mormon country, and his young heart had yearned to play a part in such adventures.

Luck was on Will's side, for by this time the wild and woolly West had become more intimately a part of the nation. As early as 1849 a stage line had been established between Santa Fé and Independence, Missouri, and not long afterward another line ran to Salt Lake City. The region between the Mississippi and California kept crying for quicker delivery of letters, newspapers, and freight and in 1854 the Federal government contracted with John Butterfield to operate his famous Overland Mail between St. Louis and San Francisco by way of El Paso. (See map, page 150.)

Meanwhile, at Leavenworth, the new firm of Russell, Majors & Waddell was using fleets of Conestoga wagons to haul heavy freight westward. In a single year this firm sent thirty-five hundred high-wheeled wagons over the trails, and employed four thousand men to convey sixteen million pounds of shipping. Eleven-year-old Will Cody, sure that he could do a man's work, begged until his mother yielded reluctantly, and off he galloped to Leavenworth to find a job with Russell, Majors & Waddell. He must have talked hard, and he must have talked

straight for soon he was signing the pledge the firm
required of all employees:

> While I am in the employ of A. Majors, I agree
> not to use profane language, not to get drunk, not to
> treat animals cruelly, and not to do anything else
> that is incompatible with the conduct of a gentleman.
> And I agree, if I violate any of the above conditions,
> to accept my discharge without any pay for my
> services.

For his keep and forty dollars a month—the
salary to be paid to his mother—Will Cody set off
on a journey to carry supplies to General Albert
Sidney Johnston who, on the basis of unsubstanti-
ated reports that Brigham Young was guilty of
"treasonable behavior," had been sent westward with
2,500 troops by the Federal government. Alfred Cum-
ming of Georgia was appointed in 1857 by the President to replace Young as governor of Utah, and, as
everyone should have expected, the Mormons rose in
rebellion. Johnston was having his hands full trying
to repress Young's followers, which certainly was no
concern of Cody's. He delivered his supplies and
counted his mission completed. Afterward an old-
timer said, "Little Billy's killed an Indian all by
himself!" Perhaps Will did kill his first Indian on
this haul, though the evidence is dubious.

What really impressed the boy was his first visit,
in 1859, to Fort Laramie, when he saw in the flesh
those legendary men of the Old West—Kit Carson
and Jim Bridger. Kit, now fifty, lived in Taos, New
Mexico but could not resist frequent trips to Lara-

mie, for wanderlust was ground into the marrow of his bones. Jim talked mountains and Indians to the boy as long as he cared to listen, which was by the hour. No one knew better than Jim the changes that had come—and were still coming thicker than mosquitoes in August—into the country that once had been the mysterious domain of the mountain men— no one, that is, unless it was the proprietors of Russell, Majors & Waddell, who were then at work on plans for opening the Pony Express. (Map, page 150.)

2.

This enterprise was breathtaking in its scope. Huge sums of money were needed, new roads must be laid (especially beyond the mountains of Nevada), eighty riders hired, hundreds of tons of grain and hay shipped to one hundred and ninety way stations attended by two hundred stationkeepers and attendants before Russell, Majors & Waddell could open faster mail service from St. Joseph, Missouri to the blue Pacific. The nature of the undertaking was not disguised in the advertisement that the firm published:

WANTED

YOUNG SKINNY WIRY FELLOWS not over eighteen. Must be expert riders willing to risk death daily. Orphans preferred. WAGES $25 per week. Apply, *Central Overland Express, Alta Bldg., Montgomery St.*

The "young skinny fellows" weighed 135 pounds at the outside. They could ride like the wind. The "stage" between stations varied from ten to twenty miles, depending on the topography of the country. A horseman, who may have ridden from forty to one hundred and twenty-five miles, only rested and chatted with the stationkeeper until the rider from the opposite direction arrived, when he seized the mail sack and went flying back to his home base. Sometimes a rider was injured—or killed by an Indian—and the waiting Pony Expressman had to carry the mail on a double stage. Happily, such emergencies were rare, and a rider rode his round only once a week—and rode it lightly, too, discarding the carbine with which he was originally equipped and carrying only a pair of revolvers and a knife. Later even these weapons were left behind.

The Mexican word *mochila* was the name given to his mailsack, which was thrown over his feather of a saddle. The mailsack contained four pockets, two in front and two in back, three of which were locked before the rider departed, for they contained the mail that was going straight through. The fourth was the "way" pocket, left open, to which mail could be added at any station. All letters were written on thin paper. The original rate for a half-ounce letter carried from the Missouri River to California was $5.00 in gold, but this rate was reduced to $2.50 and then to $1.00. Half-breed California mustangs carried the pony riders between stations. They were marvelous little animals, tougher and faster than their ancestors, the Moorish steeds, introduced into America by the Spaniards.

It was a wonderful sight when the pony rider reached a station. Sam Clemens of Hannibal, Missouri had still to win immortality as author-humorist Mark Twain on that day in 1861 in Nevada when he observed the Pony Express in action:

> In a little while all interest was taken up in stretching our necks and watching for the "pony rider"—the fleet messenger who sped across the continent from St. Joe to Sacramento, carrying letters nineteen hundred miles in eight [nine] days. . . . No matter what time of the day or night his watch came on and no matter whether it was winter or summer, raining, snowing, hailing, or sleeting, or whether his beat was a level straight road or a crazy trail over mountain crags and precipices, or whether it led through peaceful regions or regions that swarmed with hostile Indians, he must be always ready to leap into the saddle and be off like the wind! . . . The rider's dress was thin and fitted close; he wore a roundabout [jacket] and a skullcap and tucked his pantaloons into his boots like a race rider. . . . His horse was stripped of all unnecessary weight too. He wore light shoes or none at all. . . .
>
> We had a consuming desire, from the beginning, to see a pony rider, but somehow or other all that passed us managed to streak by in the night, and so we heard only a whiz and a hail, and the swift phantom of the desert was gone before we could get our heads out the windows. But now we were expecting one along every moment and would see him in broad daylight. Presently the driver exclaims:
> *"Here he comes!"*

Every neck is stretched farther and every eye strained wider. Away across the endless dead level of the prairie a black speck appears against the sky, and it is plain that it moves. Well, I should think so! In a second or two it becomes a horse and rider, rising and falling, rising and falling—sweeping toward us nearer and nearer—growing more and more distinct, more and more sharply defined—nearer and still nearer, and the flutter of the hoofs comes faintly to the ear—another instant a whoop and a hurrah from our upper deck, a wave of the rider's hand, but no reply, and man and horse burst past our excited faces and go swinging away like a belated fragment of a storm!

So sudden is it all and so like a flash of unreal fancy that, but for the flake of white foam left quivering and perishing on a mail sack after the vision had flashed by and disappeared, we might have doubted whether we had seen any actual horse and man at all, maybe.

As anyone who knew him might have expected, Will Cody was not going to be left out of this excitement. At first there was objection to Will's youthfulness, but he was given a trial on the stage between Red Buttes and Three Crossings, stations just beyond Fort Laramie. Again Will proved his mettle, once outriding fifteen Indians in a ravine, once doing double duty, when a drunken driver failed the Pony Express, and riding 320 miles in twenty-one hours and forty minutes (the longest ride on record). Cody now was fourteen and big for his age. He met Wild Bill Hickok and believed every story he told, but later Will must have known that Wild Bill was no Jim Bridger or Kit Carson.

And Will Cody must have known a great deal more. Although the Pony Express could take enormous pride in the fact that its Pony Bob (R. H. Haslam) had carried the first news to Nevada of Lincoln's election to the presidency, and although it reduced the time for transmitting letters between San Francisco and New York by ten days, its riders, waving their hats to the men stringing a transcontinental telegraph line across mountains and prairies, must have guessed that the click of its key had doomed their enterprise (see map, page 150). For eighteen months the Pony Express flourished and then, as Charles Dickens said of old Marley in *A Christmas Carol,* it was deader than a doornail.

3.

An act "To facilitate communication between the Atlantic and Pacific States by electric telegraph" was passed by Congress on June 16, 1860. Opposition to the construction of a transcontinental telegraph system often became bitter. The croakers said that the project was a waste of money, and a critic in Fort Leavenworth, Kansas gave four reasons why:

1. Poles would blow down as a result of windstorms, and the wires would break under the heavy fall of snow and the formation of ice.
2. Prairie fires would burn the poles.

3. Buffaloes would rub the poles down.

4. The Indians would cut the poles and destroy the line.

Congress, admitting that there were risks, still thought the telegraph worth trying, stipulating that the project must be completed by July 31, 1862. Surveys were made and the building began. The crews worked in three sections. In advance went a party of ten men to dig the four-foot holes for the poles. This line of men worked steadily and swiftly, each man walking about a third of a mile from the hole he had just finished to begin digging the next. Behind came another group, distributing wire and insulators. Another crew of six men nailed the brackets on the poles and raised and set them. A trimmer cut down tree branches that touched the wire.

The scene on the Plains and in the Rockies was dazzling. Seventy-five heavy wagons carried the equipment. Axes rang as trees were felled for poles. A large herd of cattle, including milch cows, was driven along to provide food. Good tents gave shelter. The cook was up at dawn, preparing breakfast and the noonday meal that the men carried on the job. Indian troubles might have multiplied had the men missed the chance, whenever they saw an Indian holding the end of a wire, to produce an artificial shock that caused the Indian to jump back and gaze upon the wire with a new respect.

Pony riders like Will Cody, waving their hats as they streaked by, saw the line take shape, and it was no surprise to them that on the date set the tele-

graph was in operation. News of the Civil War then
raging, east of the Mississippi, reached eager Californians weeks earlier than previously had been possible. And even as the cannon roared on those distant
battlefields, the Pacific Railway Act of 1862 provided
for the construction of a transcontinental railroad
by the Central Pacific and the Union Pacific, with
the Central Pacific building eastward from the California line and the Union Pacific building westward
from Council Bluffs, Iowa.

4.

The work began in earnest with the war's end.
Of course Will Cody had his part in this enterprise.
Mounted on his horse, Brigham, named for the Mormon leader, Will was now a dashing figure with hair
that he wore long and flowing. In the seventeen
months during which Will supplied meat for railroad workers, he killed 4,280 buffaloes and thereafter
would never outlive his nickname of Buffalo Bill.
Armed with his favorite gun, "Lucretia Borgia,"
he had his own style as a buffalo hunter—riding to
the head of the herd, pressing the leaders, bringing
them down one by one. Soon the herd was circling,
and he picked off each beast as it started away from
the circle.

In all phases, the construction of the transcontinental railroad was a tremendous undertaking. The
surveys made to determine where the tracks should
be laid covered twenty-five thousand miles. Thou-

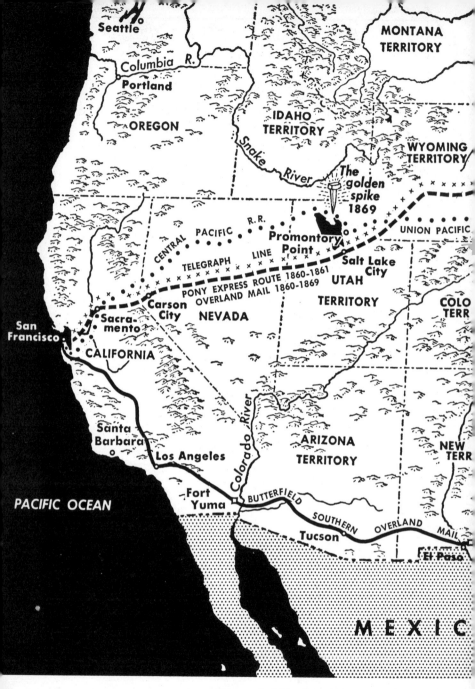

Butterfield's Southern Overland Mail
Route (———); the Pony Express (- --);

the first transcontinental railroad (. . . .);
and the transcontinental telegraph (xxxx)

sands of workers were employed, and guards fanned out to defend them against Indian attack. A large number of the laborers were Irish and a popular ditty of the day ran:

> *Then drill, my Paddies, drill—*
> *Drill, my heroes, drill—*
> *Drill all day, no sugar in your tray,*
> *Workin' on the U. P. railway.*

General Grenville M. Dodge, who had been General Sherman's engineer in the Civil War campaign against Atlanta, and was now chief engineer for the Union Pacific, described how the work progressed:

The location part in our work [that is, the surveying] on the Union Pacific was followed by the construction corps, grading generally a hundred miles at a time. That distance was graded in about thirty days on the plains, as a rule, but in the mountains we sometimes had to open our grading several miles ahead of our track in order to complete the grading by the time the track should reach it. All the supplies for this work had to be hauled from the end of the track, and the wagon transportation was enormous. At one time we were using at least ten thousand animals, and most of the time from eight to ten thousand laborers. The bridge gangs always worked from five to twenty miles ahead of the track, and it was seldom that the track waited for a bridge. To supply one mile of track with material and supplies required about forty cars, as on the plains everything—rails, ties, bridging, fastenings, all railway supplies, fuel for locomotives and trains, and supplies for men and animals on the entire work—had to be transported from the Missouri River.

Therefore, as we moved westward, every hundred miles added vastly to our transportation. Yet the work was so systematically planned and executed that I do not remember an instance in all the construction of the line of the work being delayed a single week for want of material. . . .

Track-laying became a kind of poetry to another witness:

The boarding cars go in advance. They are pushed to the extremity of the track; a construction train then runs up, unloads its material and starts back to bring another from the second line. . . . The rails within reach, parties of five men stand on either side. One in the rear throws a rail upon the rollers, three in advance seize it and run out with it to the proper distance. The chairs have, meantime, been set under the last rails placed. The two men in the rear, with a single swing, force the end of the rail into the chair, and the chief of the squad calls out 'Down,' in a tone that equals the 'Forward' to an army. Every thirty seconds there came that brave "Down," "Down," on either side the track. They were the pendulum beats of a mighty era. . . .

Indeed, an epic of industry was unfolding. The slaves who had built the Pyramids under the lash of a Pharoah's whip achieved no greater triumph. By May 2, 1866 only 40 miles of road were completed; then in the next 182 working days an additional 145 miles were laid.

The building of the transcontinental railroad, according to a pamphlet published by the Union Pacific in 1868, seemed "wonderful" to all connected with it. The pamphlet, written for parties who, at the railroad's expense, came to view the construction, described valleys as "green oceans which roll from Colorado to Indiana" beside which "the green fields of Europe are mere garden patches." Again: "Much of the land at the mouth of the valley is under cultivation, and the deep black of the loam, the dark green of the wheat, the lighter grass, the deeper shades, and the brown of that which the fires of the autumn spared, make the wide expanse a mosaic which nature alone could color . . ." And again: "Further on, huge plows, drawn by eight oxen, la-

The building of the transcontinental railroad

bored slowly along, each furrow being an added rip-
ple to the tide which is sweeping up over all these
rich regions—a tide whose ebb the youngest will
never know."

The transcontinental railroad was a superbly
American enterprise, for as it poured hundreds of
thousands of dollars into the project it also began
to sell future investors and homesteaders the oppor-
tunities which it was creating. And equally superb
was the progress made—the Central Pacific laying
down 689 miles of track, the Union Pacific 1,086
miles.

seemed wonderful to all connected with it

5.

The two roads came together at Promontory Point, Utah on May 10, 1869. That last day about one hundred feet of track were laid and, said a witness, Alexander Toponce, who seized a shovel and attempted to throw some dirt on the ties so that he could tell about it afterward, "everybody tried to take a hand in the work." It was, Toponce confessed, "a very hilarious occasion." California furnished a golden spike to complete the railroad, Nevada one of silver, and Arizona one of gold, silver, and iron, while "the last tie was of California laurel." The Governor of Arizona (who happened to be president of the Central Pacific) drove the last spike— naturally missing it entirely on the first stroke of the sledge. Toponce reported:

> What a howl went up! Chinese, Mexicans, and everybody yelled with delight. "He missed it. Yee." The engineers blew the whistles and rang their bells. Then [Governor] Stanford tried it again and tapped the spike and the [telegraph] operators had fixed their instruments so that the tap was reported in all the offices east and west, and set bells to tapping in hundreds of towns and cities. . . .

The vice-president of the Union Pacific took up the sledge, and soon everyone was howling with glee as they slapped their sides and cried: "He missed it too, yow!"

But Toponce had to admit that it was "a great occasion" when finally the two lines were joined, adding: "I do not remember now what any of the speakers said, but I do remember that there was a great abundance of champagne."

Actually, compared to Toponce's account of the scene at Promontory Point, the rest of America received this moment in a much more reverent mood. The telegraph pounded out a succession of messages to a waiting country: "Almost ready. Hats off. Prayer is being offered. . . . We have got done praying. The spike is about to be presented. . . . All ready now."

Across America people shouted, their voices blending with ringing church bells.

The life of the railroaders in those first years in the wild and woolly West was not easy. As early as 1867, the Indians had discovered that by pulling the spikes and bending the rails, they could make a locomotive jump the track and turn over. The survivors of such a wreck were easily killed. The Cheyennes, especially, found this practice great sport.

The Red Man never lacked for imagination in trying to hold onto his homeland. In the end he lost, but he made the struggle costly.

9.

THE REVOLT OF THE RED MAN:
War Ravishes the West

To the frontiersman, moving ever westward, the Indian was never a hero. Captain Eugene F. Ware, who fought with the 7th Iowa Cavalry against the Indians, belonged to this age of the frontiersman. Captain Ware never knew a good Red Man, declaring that "the wild Indian if locked up in a room would soon kill himself with his own stench, were he not used to it." And the captain added: "Horses could smell him half a mile to the windward, and civilized horses shied at him, sniffed and snorted at him, and tried to run away from him the same as from a buffalo or wild animal."

To Captain Ware, Indian men, with their beardless faces and lazy customs, seemed more like women, and Indian women, with faces hardened from years of toil, seemed more like men—a distinction that Captain Ware would never forget nor forgive. The captain granted no virtue whatever to his adversary, insisting:

> Our boys also would go into the river at the end of the day's trip, and although the Pawnees were as good in physique as any of the Indians and were picked men, they were not up to our men, who were not picked men. Our men were only average Iowa farm boys, but in physical appearance they exceeded the Indian. They had heavier shoulders and thighs, and . . . in the water with the Indians the superiority of the white soldier was manifest.

Ware served under General Robert B. Mitchell who, wounded in the early fighting of the Civil War, was sent to the Kansas country to keep order. In their attitude toward the Indian, Mitchell and Ware were as alike as peas in a pod. A lawyer from Ohio before joining the army, Mitchell brought to Kansas both loves: his strict discipline, and his weakness for arguing over how many angels could stand on the head of a pin.

When, early in the spring of 1864, Mitchell met in council with various Sioux and Pawnee chiefs, the general looked like a king, wearing a yellow sash and seating himself in a mahogany chair. When the pipe of peace was passed from the Indians to their military overlords, Mitchell took out a silk handkerchief. Carefully he wiped off the stem before taking three ceremonial puffs, giving support to a lieutenant standing nearby who muttered: "I don't believe I want to swap saliva with that crowd."

The meeting was a failure from the start. The

Mitchell met in council with various Sioux and Pawnee chiefs, looking like a king, and seating himself in a mahogany chair

chiefs spoke angrily of the white man's wagons that were invading their lands and driving away the herds on which they depended for food. The Indians boasted that the Sioux nation had twenty-six thousand organized warriors, whereas the white people in the Platte Valley numbered only a few hundred. If trouble came, they said, "we are not afraid . . . we outnumber them."

Mitchell was as inflexible as a ramrod. The Indians required too much land on which to live, he replied, and if they would adopt the customs of the white man all trouble would cease. The earth, Mitchell continued, belonged to "all the people on it." Moreover, since the Sioux had taken this land by driving westward their ancient enemies, the Chippewas, he argued that "rights to the land, if accumulated by the Indians, could be accumulated by the whites."

Both sides clearly were playing a game of bluff and counter-bluff. When the meeting ended, General Mitchell once more wiped the stem of the peace pipe with his silk handkerchief and sucked three times. He fooled no one. The Indians went away, knowing that no matter how many treaties they signed with the Great Father in Washington, the hordes of white invaders would increase.

Yet what was happening in the Platte Valley exhilarated Captain Ware:

Various persons began to tell about the [wagon] trains they had seen. Many persons told of trains from ten to fifteen miles long, being aggregations of several independent trains. . . . Mrs. MacDonald, the wife of the ranchman at our post, said she had many times kept count of the wagons which went by, and that one day they went up to nine hundred, counting those going both ways.

To the Indian, the coaches of the Overland Mail, the pony riders, the builders of the telegraph, the surveyors of future railroads, were equally awe-inspiring spectacles. His fear was understandable.

Apparently, the Civil War, being fought east of the Mississippi, did not for a moment stop the growth of the country beyond the Missouri. In December of 1862 President Lincoln told Congress: "The Territories of the United States, with unimportant exceptions, have remained undisturbed by the civil war, and they are exhibiting such evidence of prosperity as justifies an expectation that some of them will soon be in a condition to be organized as States." A year later the President sounded even more optimistic: "The mineral resources of Colorado, Nevada, Idaho, New Mexico and Arizona are proving far richer than has been heretofore understood." And in 1864 Lincoln informed Congress: "The number [of people] in organized Territories is triple now what it was four years ago."

The achievement was unbelievable—not only to Lincoln, but also to the Indian, who understood that if the invasion of the white man was not stopped, his way of life must end forever.

2.

During the years of the Civil War, the Indian tried desperately to strike back. In the North it became popular to blame the Confederacy for every massacre that occurred, but history would never support such wartime propaganda. For all that a Captain Ware and a General Mitchell might despise the Indian as a savage, the Indian took a realistic and quite civilized view toward the Civil War, seeing in these times—when white men enjoyed the sport of killing white men—an opportunity for the Red Man to put in a few licks in behalf of his own independence.

The first outbreak of war came in Minnesota in 1862 and, when early reports reached St. Paul of the massacres that had occurred along the Yellow Medicine River, no one could believe them. Then half-crazed, terrified survivors stumbled back to civilization. They told fearful stories of the outrages committed by the Sioux under the leadership of Little Crow. Children and women, escaping the carnage, babbled incoherently. Patient listening reconstructed the awful images that haunted their minds: of the heads of babies bashed against wagon wheels; of the old and sickly killed in their beds.

A military expedition under Henry H. Sibley finally crushed this uprising, and at Lincoln's order thirty-eight "Indians and half-breeds" were hung at Mankato for the atrocities committed. Stoically, the

Indians chanted a death song as they were led to the scaffold. Reported the St. Paul *Press*:

> One young yellow fellow who had been given a cigar by one of the reporters, just before marching from their quarters, was smoking it on the stand [scaffold], puffing away very coolly during the intervals of the hideous "Hi-yi-yi," "Hi-yi-yi," and even after the cap was drawn over his face, he managed to get it over his mouth and smoke.

To Eastern readers the story of the thirty-eight "Indians and half-breeds," dropping to their deaths at Mankato, ended the incident. To the Indian the "Hi-yi-yi" of their death song echoed far and wide. Around council fires they talked bitterly of the white man's greed for land, of his contempt for people who were non-white, of his destruction of the buffalo and other natural resources upon which the Indian built his way of life.

The Red Man possessed a sense of history. From the time the inhabitants of Georgia had sent the Cherokees westward so that their lands could be seized, a pattern had been established. Wherever the white man wanted a home, the Indian was expected to move on—to what end no Indian could say.

3.

In the summer of 1864, Colorado experienced a wave of Indian revolt along a stretch of four hundred miles of stagecoach route, where nearly every ranchman's family was massacred or forced to flee.

Major Jacob Downing led forty men from Denver in an expedition against the guilty Cheyennes—and led them in no peaceful mood, when they came to an Indian village near Cedar Bluffs.

"We commenced shooting," Downing remembered. "I ordered the men to commence killing them. I burnt up their lodges and everything I could get hold of. We captured about one hundred head of stock, which was distributed among the boys."

The Cheyennes struck back. Houses were burned and scalps lifted within twenty miles of Denver. Colorado's Governor Evans responded wrathfully, for without "severe chastisement," he said, there could never be peace.

Black Kettle, chief of the Cheyennes, offered to forget the past.

"You are our father," he told Governor Evans. "We want to hold you by the hand."

Evans wanted no peace. He had raised a regiment of volunteers, he said, "to kill Indians and they must kill Indians." Meanwhile Black Kettle (and his friend White Antelope, chief of the Arapahos) led some five hundred women and children of their tribes to a winter camp near Fort Lyon, believing that peace was near.

One of the greatest tragedies in American history was in the making. Its leading figure was Ohio-born Colonel John M. Chivington, an old Methodist preacher with convictions as strong as his gigantic body. Chivington was the kind of dedicated warrior who could boast to his half-breed guide, "I haven't had an Indian to eat for a long time."

In this spirit, in November of 1864, Chivington and some seven hundred troops surrounded Black Kettle's camp. The colonel ignored the American flag above the white flag that the chief ran up on the lodgepole of his tepee. Black Kettle escaped—really against his will, for he would have preferred to die with his people in the burning that followed, but White Antelope, wrapped in a blanket, sang a death song as Chivington's soldiers drove him to the ground and shot him.

Not content, the Colorado soldiers chased the Indians up Sand Creek. What followed, according to the testimony of a contemporary, was not pleasing:

All manner of depredations were inflicted on their [the Indians'] persons; they were scalped, their brains knocked out; the [white] men used knives, ripped open women, clubbed little children, knocked them on the head with their guns, beat their brains out, mutilated their bodies in every sense of the word.

The Sand Creek Massacre would write November 19, 1864 into history as a date when war to the death between Red Man and white in the wild and woolly West became almost inevitable. Old mountain men like Kit Carson and Jim Bridger threw up their hands in angry horror. No self-respecting people, which they knew the Indians to be, could tolerate such treatment. Will Cody, wearing the fringed buckskin garments that made him appear half Indian, shook his head. He knew, like Kit and Jim, what must happen.

Northward now would travel the war pipe of the Cheyennes to be smoked by the Sioux. Thereafter every wagon journeying westward would become fair game for the Indian's revenge. Overland coaches would be shot up, their way stations raided. Trains would be derailed, the cars burned, the passengers killed and scalped. Thus one tragedy had set the stage for other tragedies at the moment when the end of the Civil War freed United States troops to patrol these areas of conflict.

4.

Out of that Civil War, strutting like a peacock, came George Armstrong Custer. At the age of twenty-three, he had become the youngest brigadier general in the history of the United States, and two years later the nation's youngest major general. The adjectives that best described Custer were young and wiry, tough and intelligent. "If I were an Indian," he once wrote, "I often think that I would greatly prefer to cast my lot among those of my people who adhered to the free open plains, rather than to submit to the confined limits of a reservation, there to be the recipient of the blessed benefits of civilization, with its vices thrown in without stint or measure."

When George Armstrong Custer reached the Dakota Territory in 1874 he knew perfectly well that by treaty, fourteen years before, the Black Hills had been designated as a permanent reservation of the Sioux and Cheyennes. Nonetheless, penetrating this region, Custer rode jauntily at the head of the United States Seventh Cavalry, describing his mission as "scientific." For a long time there had been rumors that gold existed here and Custer, with his winsome smile, came back telling everyone that the facts justified the stories.

A rush of prospectors into the Black Hills followed, a sore point with the Indians. Meanwhile the Red Men, dissatisfied with the rations issued on their reservation, occasionally staged a raid on white settlements, a sore point on the other side. The army warned the Indians to remain on their reservation, but the hard winter of 1876 proved especially cruel in the Dakotas and hungry Red Men searched where they could for food.

The army believed that it must move. Aboard the steamer *Far West,* anchored off the mouth of Montana's Rosebud Creek on June 21, 1876, were Generals Alfred H. Terry, John Gibbon, and Custer. All three had fought the Confederates in the Civil War, considered themselves seasoned warriors and, as a consequence, may have underestimated the fighting ability of the Indians who now opposed them.

Anyhow, Terry, who laid the plans, sounded like a man brushing a fly from his sleeve. Gibbon, said Terry, would lead the Seventeenth Infantry up the Yellowstone, cross to the south side, march up the Bighorn and on to the Little Bighorn while Custer, with his Seventh Cavalry, drove up the Rosebud. By catching the Indians between two forces, Terry meant to compel them to fight where they could be easily crushed. Custer, issuing fifteen days of rations and ammunition to his men, agreed with the plan. He started off next day in high spirits.

Along the Little Bighorn, various Indian tribes were gathering in great strength—Northern Cheyennes, Teton Sioux, Ogallalas, Uncpapas, Minneconjous, Sans-Arcs. Chiefs, whose names had become legends, strolled through camps that covered three miles and Sitting Bull, Crazy Horse, Black Moon, and Spotted Eagle were but a few of the leaders whose presence aroused awe among their people. Some estimates place the number of tribesmen at twelve thousand, others at fifteen thousand. The warriors alone must have approached five thousand.

Custer, pushing along the Rosebud, counted his own force at six hundred soldiers in addition to forty-four Indian scouts and some twenty packers, guides, and civilians. Toward late June the scouts reported numerous Indian trails turning westward toward the valley of the Little Bighorn. Custer was persuaded to look for himself at the smoke rising from the campfires. But ground haze obscured the view that day, and Custer's mood reflected the rashness that so often marked his military conduct. Wait for Gibbon's infantrymen? Nonsense! He would strike at once and clean out these red rascals!

Custer divided his force into three battalions. One, under Captain Frederick W. Benteen, scouted the trail to the left. The other two—one under Major

Marcus A. Reno, the other under Custer—advanced along opposite banks of a creek flowing into the valley of the Little Bighorn.

Two miles from the river, when at last the encampment was sighted, bluffs and the foliage of tall cottonwood trees played tricks with Custer's vision. He never guessed how many tepees stretched before him, when he ordered Reno and his battalion to plunge straight ahead and attack the camp. Custer swung his own forces to the right, obviously intending to strike the Indians on the flank and rear in support of Reno.

Only the Indians would be able to give an account of what happened. With fearful whoops, the Indians swarmed down on Reno. Dismounting his men, the major attempted to pull back to the bluffs.

Panic took over and the engagement became a wild scramble in all directions as each man fended for himself. There was a brief view of Custer, erect in his stirrups and waving his hat in encouragement. The cries of anguish died away after a time. There was only one survivor of the brutal massacre— Comanche, Custer's horse.

5.

"Custer's Last Stand," in picture, fiction, and fact, became an American tradition. For generations, schoolboys were brought to the point of weeping over what the Indians had done to poor Custer (without ever hearing a word of what Colonel Chivington had done to the poor Indians in the Sand Creek Massacre of 1864). In the death to which his own foolish military judgment led him, Custer won his greatest victory. The nation's pride would never be satisfied now until, once and for all, the white man had prevailed over the red.

A long struggle ensued. In New Mexico and Arizona, the Apache chieftain, Geronimo, left his own trail of terror. Named Goyathlay, meaning "One Who Yawns," Geronimo took the name that came down in history from the Spanish word Jerome. He was born about June, 1829 in Arizona and, growing up, learned two useful arts: stealing and "feats of war." Mexicans killed his mother, wife, and children in 1858. Geronimo vowed vengeance against all white men thereafter, and his intelligence made him, as a result, the most effective Indian leader in the Southwest.

The Federal government's efforts in the mid-1880's to keep the Indians from brewing an intoxicating drink called *tiswin* gave Geronimo the cause he wanted. Red Men rallied to the defense of this liberty, enabling Geronimo to leave death and destruction wherever he rode. Captured by General George Crook in 1886, Geronimo, agreeing to a truce, quickly violated this pledge and fled across the border. Pursued relentlessly by an expedition under General Nelson A. Miles, the Apache terrorist finally was cornered in the mountainous regions of Arizona's Skeleton Canyon. Geronimo surrendered on September 3, 1886; then, accepting Christianity, lived peacefully until his death in 1909.

Mining centers, Indian reservations and battles, and

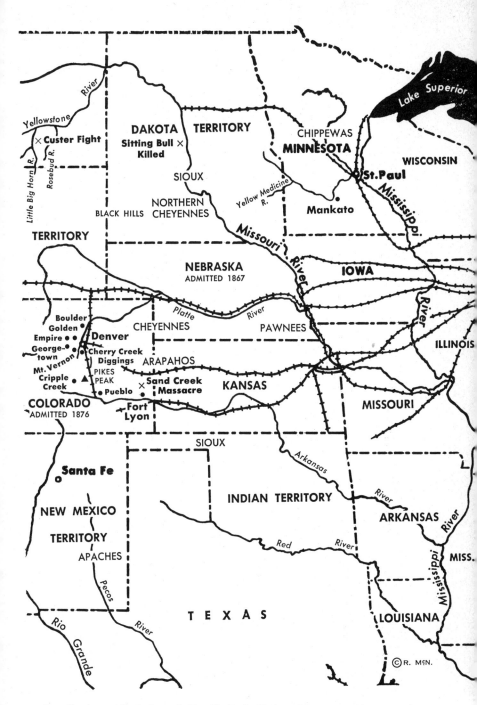

territories and states of the United States (1862–1886)

Meanwhile, in the North, miners and ranchers, coming into the fertile valleys of Idaho, produced trouble with the Indians that in 1877 exploded into a war with the Nez Percés. In French the name of these robust Red Men meant "Pierced Nose," and their leader, Chief Joseph, ranked with the best Indian statesmen of the Plains.

Federal troops, who were roundly defeated in White Bird Canyon and later outfoxed by the Nez Percés in seeking a battle on the Clearwater, could only respect (if grudgingly) the sagacity and wisdom of their foe. Eventually, near the Canadian border of Montana, the might of the Federal forces prevailed. With the Nez Percés surrounded, Chief Joseph spoke to his people and to history:

I am tired of fighting. Our chiefs are killed. Looking Glass is dead. Toolhulhulsote is dead. The old men are all dead. It is the young men who say yes or no. He [they] who led the young men are all dead. It is cold and we have no blankets. The little children are freezing to death. My people, some of them, have run away to the hills and have no blankets, no food. No one knows where they are—perhaps freezing to death.

I want to have time to look for my children and see how many of them I can find. Maybe I shall find them among the dead. Hear me, my chiefs. I am tired. My heart is sick and sad. I will fight no more forever.

Wars always are lost before the battles cease. After the Nez Percés surrendered, the Bannocks tried to carry on the struggle until their leader, Buffalo Horn, was killed.

6.

As Chief Joseph spoke his tragic words, "I am tired . . . I will fight no more forever," a few Americans were awakening to the fact that they had treated the Red Man unfairly. Buffalo Bill was now a successful producer in the East, with his Wild West shows, so that the struggle passed beyond those who had seen the wild and woolly West grow up, to a woman born in 1830 in Amherst, Massachusetts and who came west to escape the memory of the tragic death of her first husband and child.

Her name was Helen Hunt Jackson. Visiting the Indians on their reservations, she became indignant over the government's neglect of these stepchildren. Diligently she studied the problems of the Indians and then wrote a report, entitled *A Century of Dishonor,* which in 1881 she distributed to the members of Congress at her own expense.

For the first time, many Americans recognized the fact that they may have dealt unfairly with the Red Man. The following year the Indian Rights Association was organized; a year later the Lake Mohonk Conference of Friends of the Indians was founded; and the legislatures of six states—Maine, Connecticut, New York, Pennsylvania, Delaware, and Michigan—sent memorials to Congress demanding improved conditions for Indians on reservations.

But reform came slowly. Long before then the last part of the West had been opened to the unbridled scramble of homesteaders.

10.

THE WINNING OF THE WEST:
The Sodbusters

In only a few minutes now the New Year of 1863 would reach Nebraska Territory. The dancers shouted and stomped their feet as a red-faced fiddler sawed away at his favorite tunes—"Turkey in the Straw" and "Soapsuds over the Fence." A bit grumpily the land office agent stopped dancing when told there was a fellow outside who wished to see him.

The caller's name was Daniel Freeman, and he came on serious business. At shortly after midnight he wanted to file the first land claim in Nebraska Territory under the Homestead Act. Grumbling, the land office agent went off to do his duty, and so missed the wild outburst of fiddling that welcomed the New Year, but Daniel Freeman was happy. He had officially obtained his 160 acres near the present town of Beatrice and found a niche in history as Nebraska's first "sodbuster" (farmer).

Perhaps it was true, as someone said, that you couldn't tell the truth about the West without lying, and certainly the sodbuster's story fitted that pattern. At times he seemed to endure simply because he did not possess the sense to quit. Yet wherever there was free land to claim, sodbusters came to grab it— first by the hundreds, then by the thousands—until suddenly they appeared to gobble up everything within sight.

Often they were found where they had no business being, as in the case of the "boomers" who sneaked into the fertile ranges of Oklahoma and against whom, for years, Federal troops carried on a hit-and-run kind of warfare. But the boomer was tricky and persistent and the National government gave in. Two million acres of land were purchased from the Indians in central Oklahoma and April 22, 1889 was selected as the day when this tract would be opened to homesteaders.

2.

The reporter for the St. Louis *Globe Democrat* who went to Arkansas City, Kansas, to see what a land rush was like, decided that it was unlike anything else on earth. Thousands "of seekers of something for nothing" wandered all night through the streets, waiting for sun-up of the fateful day. Although the depot was jammed till the walls bulged, all night the railroads kept running in extra trains and dumping new hordes on Arkansas City. Ticket

sales to Arthur and Guthrie, the nearest town sites,
kept the place a constant madhouse.

The reporter watched and shook his head:

Every one seemed to be talking, and there was a
perfect babel, but the grand rush commenced about
six, when the people who had slept uptown joined
their less fortunate brethren. Some carried absolute-
ly nothing in their hands, evidently thinking they
could do the rushing better for not being handi-
capped. But a marked characteristic of the crowd
was the great number of spades and axes carried.

Prudently the railroad refused to announce
which train was scheduled to leave first, which was
just as well, or the axes might have been used in a
battle for seats. Of course there was not enough room
for everyone, even though several flatcars were fitted
with plank seats. Men tried to ride on the cow-
catchers of the locomotives, were chased away, and
sneaked back.

At twelve-fifteen o'clock—the time set for the
start of the rush—the whistles of the engines
screeched loudly. Men cheered, cried, remained silent,
since emotion takes many forms. The trains chugged
off, and fifty yards inside Oklahoma, the first passenger leaped off. The reporter from St. Louis
watched him: "He fell pretty heavily but was on his
feet in a few seconds, collected his baggage, which he
had thrown out ahead, and was turning sods before
the train was out of sight."

Not without reason would Oklahoma be nick-
named "The Sooner State," for there were those who
had invaded the territory *sooner* than the law al-

There was a perfect babel . . . a marked characteristic of the crowd was the great number of spades and axes carried

lowed. The St. Louis man saw them: ". . . squatters pure and simple now came in view. They sprang out of the woods on every side, and it was evident from the appearance of some of them that they had been in hiding for weeks. . . ."

3.

Truly, the "fun" had begun. A reporter for the New York *Tribune* called the rush into Oklahoma "the greatest race ever seen in the world," contested on "a racetrack 100 miles wide" with "a principality for the stake." By train, by wagon, by bicycle, on foot, the boomers sped forward. One of the *Tribune* man's most vivid recollections was of "Miss Mabel Gentry, of Thayer, Neosho County, Kans., who rode a fiery little black pony at the full jump for the seven miles from the [starting] line to the town site of Kildare, reaching that point in seventeen minutes. It was a terrible drive from start to finish."

In the crispy grass of the prairies the bicycle riders never really had a chance. Back on the train out of Arkansas City, the man from the *Globe Democrat* reported another unforgettable sight:

As the train went on toward the [first] depot the passengers kept jumping off. The town-lot craze seemed to lend speed even to cripples. A man with a wooden leg was among the first to make the dangerous jump, and held his own in the race.

All had one notion: to drive a stake into a lot, then rush off to the land office to file their claim. The reporter from St. Louis recalled:

. . . Altogether ten trains got in before three o'clock, and making allowance for those who went on to Oklahoma City, there must have been at least six thousand people in Guthrie three hours after the Territory was legally opened for settlement. It was wonderful, the manner in which disputes among the newcomers were settled in this early part of the proceedings. Sometimes half a dozen men would pounce on a lot simultaneously or nearly so. Each would commence to stake out, but after a little while a general agreement would be come to, and every applicant but one would rush off and secure an undisputed lot. There has been so far no unpleasantness of any kind.

Speculation in town lots commenced at once. Hacks met the trains and drivers shouted, "This way for lots at a dollar apiece!"

For a dollar lot hunters were driven to vacant lots and left to get their dollar's worth themselves.

The Oklahoma land rush did not quench the hunger of the homesteaders, and the National government tried once again to do so in 1893, when it purchased the Cherokee Strip. The correct name for this last part of the West to be opened for settlement was "the Cherokee Outlet." It comprised a stretch of prairie country about sixty miles wide and two hundred miles long, bounded on the north by Kansas and on the south by the then four-year-old Oklahoma Territory.

What happened then was thoroughly familiar: people stayed up all night with the "idea" gradually penetrating "the deluded crowd that this was to be a race, not a prairie schooner parade to a happy new

home." The railroad engines were fired up and ready
to go, when at noon next day the signal was given for
the start of the rush. Some estimates place the number of persons lined up on the Kansas border at one
hundred thousand.

Seth K. Humphrey, who took part in the rush
into the Cherokee Strip, remembered:

> Viewed from out in front the waiting line [the
> rush] was a breathtaking sight. We had seen it only
> from within the crowd or from the rear. The back of
> the line was ragged, incoherent; the front was even,
> smooth, solid. It *looked* like the line-up that it was. I
> thought I had sensed the immensity of the spectacle,
> but that one moment out in front gave me the un-
> matched thrill of an impending race with six thou-
> sand starters in sight.
>
> First in the line was a solid bank of horses;
> some had riders, some were hitched to gigs, buck-
> boards, carts, and wagons, but to the eye there were
> only the two miles of tossing heads, shiny chests,
> and restless front legs of horses. The medley of
> grotesque speed outfits, the stupendous gamble, the
> uniqueness of the farce and the tragedy of it—these
> were submerged in the acute expectancy of a horse
> race beyond words, incomparable.

The signal was fired and Seth and his brother
stood "in a crash of vehicles whizzing past us like a
calamity." He recalled:

> The funniest of all the starters was the engine
> with its ten carloads of men. From our stand fifty
> feet directly in front of it I was contemplating it as
> the chief absurdity of the race when the rush began.
> The engine tooted incessantly and labored hard, but

of course she could not get under way with anything like the quickness of the horses. They left her as good as tied to her cattle train. The incongruity of starting a contrivance like that with a lot of horses and calling it a race made us laugh—not only because she waddled behind so ridiculously at the start but because we knew that the crowd aboard intended to be far ahead of the horsemen long before the finish of the race, if moral suasion or cash inducement could make the old girl cough a little faster than the rules allowed.

Later Seth and his brother had to laugh at themselves. Mounted on bicycles, they found that the sharp stubble left by a prairie fire and a strong head wind slowed them down to a walk so that by six o'clock they had covered only twenty miles. That night the brilliant starlight overhead emphasized the velvet blackness of the surrounding darkness until shots rang out and angry voices cried: "Number— section—township—range—. Keep off and get off!"

One homesteader, driven off his claim that night, told the Humphrey brothers: "I wouldn't live here next to such neighbors, anyway."

Seth understood that the gun-toters were not sodbusters—farming was their last interest in life— and all they wanted was land to sell to future sodbusters. Seth was quite philosophical about the entire situation: "In the Cherokee Strip was to be repeated the history of every move into the prairie frontier: a first crop of settlers, mostly fly-by-nights, followed by a second contingent, composed largely of true farmers."

4.

They were an incredible breed, these sodbusters —as singleminded in purpose as mountain men in quest of beaver pelts, as steadfast in search of a brighter future as the gold seekers, as much in love with the rolling country as ranchmen and sheepherders. They had the courage to endure—they had to have this quality to the point where it amounted to plain stubbornness.

There was, for example, that disastrous midsummer of 1874 when the grasshopper plague struck the settlers on the High Plains of the Rocky Mountains. Stuart Henry described what happened when the grasshoppers "ate up every bit of green vegetation from the Rocky Mountains to and beyond the Missouri River":

> . . . I recall that when coming home late one afternoon for supper I stepped back surprised to see what became known as Rocky Mountain locusts covering the side of the house. Already inside, they feasted on curtains. Clouds of them promptly settled down on the whole country—everywhere, unavoidable. People set about killing them to save gardens, but this soon proved ridiculous. Specially contrived machines, pushed by horses, scooped up the hoppers in grain fields by the barrelful to burn them. This, too, was then nonsensical. Vast hordes, myriads. In a week grain fields, gardens, shrubs, vines, had been eaten down to the ground or to the bark. Nothing could be done. You sat by and saw everything go.

The word "Kansas" stood for "people of the south wind," and now that wind, dry and hot, added

to the destruction and discomfort. Wells and springs
gave out. Creeks evaporated to mere trickles. Unable
to work, farmers loafed around home until nagging
wives drove them off to town. Stuart Henry remembered:

> . . . Fathers dreaded to face their children, who
> grew raggeder. As for their dirtiness, who, you
> might almost ask, hardly dared spare water to wash
> them? Husbands hated to go home to meals, for they
> must meet the appeals of their wives to climb on
> wagons and strike out for back home.
>
> "Sell for what you can get, John—give it away—
> leave it—only let's get out. I don't have to ride on a
> railroad. A schooner headed east looks awful good to
> me."

But John didn't sell; there was something in his
sodbuster's heart that wouldn't let him. From the
East people sent free seed to help him start again,
and it seemed downright un-American to walk out
under those circumstances. So John prayed, and
scratched new furrows in the dusty ground, and
planted the seeds of charity. And 1875 brought ample
crops, good prices. John's swelling pride virtually
popped the buttons on his shirt.

5.

The first sod houses that appeared on the plains
of Kansas may not have been structures of beauty,
but at least they were cheap. Homesteader Howard
Ruede made a list of his costs in 1877: "Ridgepole
and hauling (including two loads of firewood) $1.50;

The first sod houses may not have been structures of beauty, but at least they were cheap

rafters and straw, 50c; 2 lb. nails, 15c; hinges, 20c; window 75c; total cash paid, $4.05. Then there was $4 worth of lumber, which was paid for in work, and $1.50 for hauling it over, which, together with hauling the firewood, 50c, makes $10.05 for a place to live in and firewood enough to last all summer.''

Who needed much money? Cash belonged to the future when the sodbusters had made their homesteads prosper. Neighbor helped neighbor and a community house-raising was a social event no right-minded citizen would miss. In the affable spirit of the occasion one man told another: ''Bring along the old woman and the kids.''

They all came. Together they toiled to get the work finished. Gustaf Unonius, a Swedish immigrant, marveled at the easy-going hospitality of a homesteader's life:

> . . . By four o'clock in the afternoon the work on our house had been completed, and in addition our friends had helped us saw out a door opening and two other openings on either side of that for windows. There stood now the skeleton of our place, 12 feet high, 22 feet long, and 18 feet wide. However plain and lacking in promise of comfort it may have appeared, it was the beginning of *our* home, built from logs we had cut ourselves, and so in a special sense the work of our own hands. . . .
> The work had proceeded cheerfully and heartily. Those whose job it was to lift the logs had plenty of time to tell one funny story after another. Many adventures were told from early pioneer days. Jokes, witticisms, and laughter were the order of the day.

A jug of whiskey had been placed by the side of a pail of fresh spring water with a teacup ready at hand to be used in mixing a strengthening drink. When we took leave of one another, no one was drunk. . . .

What kept the sodbuster going? Unquestionably his faith—not alone in himself, but also in God, for he was a deeply religious man. The words of " 'Tis the Old Time Religion" suited his spirit perfectly:

> *It was good enough for Father,*
> *It was good enough for Father,*
> *It was good enough for Father,*
> *And it's good enough for me.*

His life was busy and active—he needed neither motion pictures nor television to fill *his* day. The wisdom of people and what was in their hearts and minds was also in the heart and mind of Abraham Lincoln on that September day in 1859 when he addressed the Wisconsin State Fair:

> . . . Every blade of grass is a study; and to produce two, where there was but one, is both a profit and a pleasure. And not grass alone; but soils, seeds, and seasons—hedges, ditches, and fences, draining, droughts, and irrigation—plowing, hoeing, and harrowing—reaping, mowing, and threshing—saving crops, pests of crops, diseases of crops, and what will cure them—implements, utensils, and machines, their relative merits, and how to improve them—hogs, horses, and cattle—sheep, goats, and poultry—trees, shrubs, fruits, plants, and flowers—the thousand things of which these are specimens—each a world of study within itself.

The sodbuster, his children, and their children in turn made of each part of the homesteader's life a "world of study within itself." With time, sod home and log cabin were changed into comfortable, rambling farmhouse. The reaper followed the iron plow and, on plains and prairies where once "the buffalo roamed," sprang up vast oceans of wheat, corn, alfalfa, and other crops—and all protected, despite early quarrels with cattlemen and sheep herders, by fences that were "pig tight, horse high, and bull strong." Villages became towns, and towns became cities, and eventually the roads from one-room schoolhouses led to great state universities.

6.

And so with the years the wild and woolly West was tamed. Rancher and sodbuster today are alike men of vast scientific knowledge. True, deep in mountain streams, you can still find a few hardy, grizzled old fellows with their spades and pans, waiting for the strike that will make them rich, but the mining breed is dwindling. Bat Masterson, Wild Bill Hickok, Wyatt Earp—yes, even Billy the Kid and Old Calam'—may bear little resemblance to reality as we see them today on television, but then, as we admitted earlier in this chapter, it is difficult to tell the truth about the West without lying. And there are still lonely cowboys riding the range and singing ruefully:

All day on the prairie in a saddle I ride,
Not even a dog, boys, to trot by my side;
My fire I must kindle with chips gathered round
And boil my own coffee without being ground.
I wash in a pool and I wipe on a sack;
I carry my wardrobe all on my back;
For want of an oven I cook bread in a pot,
And sleep on the ground for want of a cot.

Pleasant dreams, old friend. That whistle you hear in the distance is not of one Indian brave summoning another, but of a great transcontinental passenger train humming its way westward. Among those stars overhead are the blinking lights of planes soaring to the Coast. It was the forebears of your breed, old friend, who built this country and welded America into the enormous nation that it is.

INDEX

PRINTED IN U.S.A.